THE MONETARY APPROACH TO
EXTERNAL ADJUSTMENT

By the same author

MONETA, CAMBIO E BILANCIA
DEI PAGAMENTI

The Monetary Approach to External Adjustment

A Case Study of Italy

Giuseppe Tullio

Foreword by
Paolo Baffi

St. Martin's Press New York

To my wife Dominique

 For information, write:
St. Martin's Press, Inc., 175 Fifth Avenue, New York, N.Y. 10010
Printed in Hong Kong
First published in the United States of America in 1981

ISBN 0–312–54416–2

Library of Congress Cataloging in Publication Data

Tullio, Giuseppe, 1948–
The monetary approach to external adjustment.

Updated and revised translation of Moneta, cambio e bilancia dei pagamenti.
Includes index.
1. Balance of payments—Italy. 2. Foreign exchange problem—Italy. 3. Monetary policy—Italy. I. Title.
HG3883.I8T8413 1980 382.1′7′0945
ISBN 0–312–54416–2 80–7472

Contents

List of Tables viii
List of Figures ix
Foreword by Paolo Baffi xi
Acknowledgements xiii
Introduction xiv

Chapter 1 Aspects of Balance-of-Payments and Exchange-Rate Theory in Italian Economic Thought 1
1.1 Basic assumptions and implications of the monetary approach 3
1.2 The existence of an implicit or explicit long-run demand for money 7
1.3 Arbitrage and the law of one price 10
1.4 The law of the natural distribution of money and the stability of equilibrium 11
1.5 The effects of monetary policy on the balance of payments and the exchange rate, and the neutrality of devaluation 14
1.6 The direct-expenditure effect versus the price-specie flow 19
1.7 Conclusions 21
Appendix 1.1 The long-run effect of monetary policy on the level of foreign exchange reserves 23
Appendix 1.2 The direct-expenditure effect versus the price-specie flow 25
Notes 28

Chapter 2 Fluctuations of the Italian Balance of Payments, 1951–73: An Econometric Analysis 30
2.1 Empirical tests of the Italian balance of payments 31

2.2 Alternative tests of the Italian balance of payments 44
2.3 Conclusions 49
Appendix 2.1 Symbols and sources of data used 51
Appendix 2.2 Tentative calculation of the expected size of the coefficients of the independent variables in the balance-of-payments equations of Section 2.1 53
Notes 54

Chapter 3 The Money Supply Process, Development of Financial Markets and Objectives of Italian Monetary Policy: 1960–78 57
3.1 The shift in the objectives of monetary policy 58
3.2 The money supply process in Italy 60
3.3 Main developments in Italian financial markets: 1960–78 65
3.4 Reaction function of the Italian monetary authorities (1960–5, 1966–73, 1974–8) 70
3.5 Conclusions 80
Notes 82

Chapter 4 Fluctuations in the Exchange Rate of the Lira and Swiss Franc: 1973–8 84
4.1 The monetary approach to flexible exchange rates 85
4.2 Empirical tests 89
4.3 The lira exchange-rate crisis of January–May 1976 92
4.4 Conclusions 93
Appendix 4.1 Symbols and sources of data used 94
Notes 95

Chapter 5 Speed of Adjustment of the Capital and the Current Accounts to Money Market Disturbances: Some Empirical Findings 97
5.1 Explanation of the current account: the monetary approach versus the Cambridge view 98
5.2 The model 101
5.3 Reaction pattern of the Italian capital and current accounts to monetary disturbances under fixed exchange rates 104

5.4 An extension to the flexible exchange-rate period, and conclusions 107
Appendix 5.1 List of symbols and sources of data used 111
Notes 112

Bibliography 114
Index 124

List of Tables

Table

2.1	Two-stage least-square estimates of the parameters in equations (5) and (6). Italian balance of payments. Annual data, 1951–73	36
2.2	Two-stage least-square estimates of the parameters in equations (7) and (8). Italian balance of payments. Quarterly data	40
2.3	Ordinary least-square estimates of equation (11). Annual data, 1950–73	45
2.4	Long-run elasticities of demand for money and demand deposits (from Table 2.3)	46
2.5	Italian balance of payments on *ex ante* flow-excess demand for money. Annual data, 1951–73	47
2.6	Italian balance of payments on *ex post* flow-excess demand for money. Annual data, 1951–73	48
2.7	Italian balance of payments on excess demand for money. Quarterly data, 1961–I to 1973–III	49
3.1	Reaction function of Italian monetary authorities: changes in domestic assets of the Bank of Italy. Quarterly data	74
3.2	Reaction function of Italian monetary authorities: changes in claims on government. Quarterly data	75
3.3	Reaction function of Italian monetary authorities: changes in claims on commercial banks. Quarterly data	76
4.1	Spread between the lira and Swiss franc exchange rate for banknotes (*e*) and cable transfers (*eo*) in Zurich. Monthly data, Feb. 1973–Dec. 1978	88
4.2	Rates of increase of Italian M_2 and Swiss M_1. Annualised rates	93
5.1	Italian capital movements on excess demand for money. Quarterly data, 1964–71	103
5.2	Italian current account balance, seasonally adjusted, on excess demand for money	105
5.3	Italian current account balance, seasonally adjusted, on excess demand for money. Quarterly data, 1972–8	108

List of Figures

Figure

2.1 Italian balance of payments (billions of lire). Regression 2, Table 2.1 38

2.2 Italian quarterly balance of payments (billions of lire). Regression 5, Table 2.2 42

2.3 Italian quarterly balance of payments (billions of lire). Regression 6, Table 2.2 43

3.1 Total net issues of bonds as a fraction of GDP 66

3.2 Net issues of bonds by supplier (as percentage of total issues) 67

3.3 Medium- and long-term bonds purchased by households are enterprises as a fraction of GDP and real interest rate on Treasury bonds 69

3.4 Treasury bills purchased by households and enterprises as a fraction of GDP and real interest rate on Treasury bills 70

3.5 Quarterly changes in domestic assets of the Bank of Italy and Treasury financing requirement (1960–5) 77

3.6 Quarterly changes in domestic assets of the Bank of Italy and Treasury financing requirement (1966–73) 78

3.7 Quarterly changes in domestic assets of the Bank of Italy and Treasury financing requirement (1974–8) 79

4.1 Coefficients of current and lagged $\ln M_I - \ln M_{CH}$ Regression 2, Table 4.1 90

4.2 Actual and estimated values of the spread between the lira and Swiss franc exchange rate for banknotes and cable transfers. Regression 2, Table 4.1. Feb. 1973–Dec. 1978 91

5.1 Time profile of the effects of monetary disequilibrium on the capital and the current accounts under fixed exchange rates (as percentage of total effect) 106

5.2 Italian current account balance, seasonally adjusted, billions of lire: 1962–III to 1971–IV. Estimated values obtained from regression 3, Table 5.2 107

5.3	Time profile of the effects of the monetary disequilibrium on the current account under fixed and flexible exchange rates (as percentage of total effect)	109
5.4	Italian current account balance, seasonally adjusted, billions of lire: 1972–II to 1978–IV. Estimated values obtained from regression 4, Table 5.3	110

Foreword

In recent years a school of thought has been developing in Anglo-American economic literature which has been labelled the 'monetary approach to the balance of payments and the exchange rate'. It bears a close resemblance to the monetary theory that dominated both English and Italian economic literature before the Keynesian revolution. At the risk of grossly oversimplifying, one can say that its main contribution lies in a revaluation of the role of money and of the tendency toward equilibrium of monetary and financial markets in the analysis of fluctuations of the balance of payments and the exchange rate, which post-Keynesian theories had pushed into the background. The monetary approach to the balance of payments and the exchange rate was largely developed at the University of Chicago, where Dr Tullio did his graduate work.

The present volume allies itself with this school and contains a series of essays on the Italian balance of payments and exchange rate in the post-war period. The volume is an important contribution to the literature for at least three reasons. In the first place, although the proponents of the monetary approach have emphasised the close links of their view with the balance-of-payments and exchange-rate theory of classical and neo-classical English economists, they have neglected the work of the Italian economists who, over more than three centuries from Antonio Serra to Costantino Bresciani-Turroni, developed a very similar theory. The first chapter of this book is aimed at bringing to the attention of an English-speaking audience the originality and depth of the classical Italian tradition. Of particular interest is the fact that Italian economists seemed to rely more heavily on the so-called 'direct expenditure effect' in the adjustment of the balance of payments than on Hume's price-specie flow.

Secondly, as someone who has been involved from a practical point of view with our balance of payments and exchange rate and is old enough to have participated, in the post-war period, first in the long period of stability and development and then in the one, still in progress, of inflation, instability, and slow growth, I cannot but observe that changes in money and liquidity are influenced less by the technical decisions of the central bank than by the actions of society as a whole, and in particular by decisions relating to the renewal of labour contracts and to the size of the public-sector deficit. After having analysed at length the influence of money on the balance of payments and the exchange rate, the author raises the more difficult question: 'What determines monetary expansion?' Being well aware of the above-mentioned constraints on the behaviour of the central bank, he devotes the third chapter largely to an analysis of the role of the government budget deficit in the growth of money and contrasts the experience of the period of greater stability with that of recent years.

Thirdly, the essays in this book enrich and stimulate the current debate on the constraint which the balance of payments and the exchange rate imposes on the growth of our economy. Of particular interest in this connection is the measurement of the speed of adjustment of variables like the balance of payments, the exchange rate, the current and the capital accounts to expansions or restrictions of the liquidity of the system.

Rome, June 1978 PAOLO BAFFI

Acknowledgements

I am extremely grateful to Harry G. Johnson, who, as chairman of my thesis committee at the University of Chicago, carefully read various versions of the manuscript and made numerous suggestions for its improvement. In 1975 he encouraged me to devote the introductory chapter of my dissertation to the views of the ancient Italian economists on the determination of the balance of payments and exchange rate, while in 1976, about a year before his premature death, he encouraged me to prepare a draft of a book and to add new chapters on the flexible exchange-rate period to the existing material on this theme in the dissertation. Without his help, both as a teacher and as chairman of my thesis committee, this book would not have been written.

I am also particularly grateful to Robert Z. Aliber for equally stimulating suggestions and continuing encouragement. I also would like to thank Paolo Baffi, Giorgio Basevi, Filippo Cesarano, Giovanni Cristini, Rudiger Dornbusch, Jacob Frenkel, Michele Fratianni, Rainer Masera, Maria Teresa Salvemini, Paolo Savona, Andrea Sommariva, and Paolo Sylos Labini, for help at various stages of the work.

I acknowledge the financial assistance of the *Fondazione Luigi Einaudi* and the *Ente per gli Studi Monetari e Finanziari Luigi Einaudi*. I should also like to express my gratitude to the Bank of Italy for affording me the opportunity to complete and improve the work started in Chicago in a very stimulating environment.

GIUSEPPE TULLIO

Introduction

Four of the five essays published in this book analyse various aspects of the recent re-formulation of classical balance-of-payments and exchange-rate theory which has been labelled the 'monetary approach to the balance of payments and the exchange rate', with reference to Italian experience in the post-war period. The first chapter contains an analysis of the balance-of-payments and exchange-rate theory of leading Italian economists of the last three and a half centuries or so.

The publication of the essays in English may be justified by the relatively little that is known outside Italy of both these aspects of the Italian tradition. In the case of the developments of the post-war period, an interpretation is provided which is in line with the monetary approach.

Before summarising briefly the content of this book it is perhaps useful to spend a few words on the theories which compete with the monetary approach, in order to highlight their differences and place them in historical perspective.

Until about the 1930s the prevailing balance-of-payments theory was that known as the 'price-specie flow', an application of the classical principles of monetary theory to the open economy. In English economic literature it is generally attributed to David Hume (1752). The same classical principles of monetary theory, applied to a world in which exchange rates are flexible, provides an explanation of the exchange rate, which is known as the 'purchasing-power parity theory'; this theory is generally linked to the name of Gustav Cassel (1922).

The increase in unemployment and the competitive devaluations of the 1930s stimulated the development of new theories of the balance of payments or the exchange rate, among which should be mentioned the 'elasticity approach', the 'foreign trade multiplier theory', and the absorption approach'. However, towards the end of the 1950s, the evolution of Western economies towards employment conditions which resembled those prevailing before the Depression, gave rise to a renewed interest in classical theories, an interest that was further stimulated by the acceleration of world inflation towards the end of the 1960s. The rediscovery of the classical tradition and its re-formulation to adapt it to the changed structure of the international and national monetary systems was due in large measure to Harry Johnson (1958, 1973) and Robert Mundell (1968, 1971), and to a number of their students at the University of Chicago. It is, however, important to note that the classical tradition had also remained alive elsewhere, in particular at the International Monetary Fund (1977). As far as contributions to the Italian literature are concerned the names of Costantino Bresciani-Turroni (1954) and Paolo Baffi (1968) should be mentioned.

The *elasticity approach* yields a condition under which a devaluation improves the trade balance when the supplies of exports and imports are infinitely elastic (which implies that there exist some unemployed resources in the economy). This condition is known as the 'Marshall-Lerner condition'. The elasticity approach assumes that the prices of exports expressed in domestic currency and the prices of imports expressed in foreign currency are not modified by the devaluation. This implies in turn that the products of each country are highly differentiated from one another, a belief probably not unrelated to the more or less contemporaneous development of the theory of monopolistic competition. The separation of national markets implied by the elasticity approach does not seem to be consistent with today's degree of commercial integration of western economies and in particular of European economies; although noticeable oligopolistic elements remain in the markets for some products, the tendency of price levels of traded goods to converge has been high in the post-war period, at least until exchange rates were fixed.

The Marshall-Lerner condition can also be interpreted as the stability condition of the foreign exchange market, when capital movements are assumed non-existent (Haberler, 1949).

One of the main shortcomings of the elasticity approach is that it reflects a partial equilibrium view of the working of the economic system, thus neglecting the effects of trade imbalances on the equilibrium of monetary and financial markets (and hence neglecting the importance of the monetary policy pursued by the authorities). In addition, it does not take into account the effect of a depreciation on the level of income, which is very important because it changes the position of the demand curve of imports and the supply curve of exports. It follows that it is not very useful to state a condition under which a devaluation improves the trade balance in terms of elasticities measured along curves, when the curves themselves shift following the devaluation. If one considers the effect of income changes on the position of the curves, one obtains a new condition in which the income elasticity of demand for imports also appears (Harberger, 1950), but this is not by itself sufficient to affect the partial equilibrium nature of the approach.

Although the elasticity approach has some intuitive appeal in a situation of mass unemployment, it is extremely misleading when applied to full-employment or near full-employment conditions, because the neglect of money and monetary policy become more serious.

As already observed, the elasticity approach deals only with the trade balance (or the current account). It is therefore not applicable to the analysis of the overall balance of payments or of reserve flows, whose fluctuations should interest central bankers more than those of its various components.

The *foreign trade multiplier theory* (Machlup, 1943), although offering useful insights into the adjustment mechanism of the current account, is also based on certain assumptions that make it hardly applicable to today's conditions. The theory explains only the current account and not the overall balance of payments; it neglects the importance of money and of monetary policy by normally assuming that the central bank pursues a passive monetary policy by fixing the interest rate; furthermore, it does not distinguish between stocks and flows, a distinction which is particularly important because the theories that neglect it tend to commit the error of believing that a disequilibrium in the current account on the trade balance can repeat itself for period after period without setting in motion equilibrating forces. It is in this area that the 'monetary approach' differs most clearly from competing theories (Johnson, 1976), including to a lesser extent the 'absorption approach'.

An important contribution of the early post-war period was the classic article by Alexander (1952) in which he developed the *absorption approach*, which has been incorporated and occupies a central role in the monetary approach. Alexander pointed out that if a devaluation is to create a current-account surplus it must cause a wedge between income and expenditure. One of the mechanisms that might help to create this wedge is the destruction of real cash balances brought about by a devaluation. The monetary approach extends the importance of the wedge between income and expenditure to the explanation of the balance of payments as a whole, and investigates in greater detail the role of the cash-balance effect and its relationship with the money-supply process.

An expenditure function of the type $C = Y + \alpha[M^s - M^d]$, where Y is Money income, M^s the quantity of money in nominal terms, M^d the desired quantity of money and α an adjustment coefficient, is widely used in monetary approach literature. It has been introduced by Prais (1961), and Dornbusch and Mussa (1975) have shown that it can be derived from inter-temporal utility maximising the behaviour of individuals. In the models in which financial assets also appear explicitly alongside money, the wedge between income and expenditure has to be related to the excess supply of all financial assets.

By focusing on the current account, the absorption approach emphasises the accumulation (or decumulation) of all financial assets, while the monetary approach leaves below the line only monetary movements. Thus, they can be considered to some extent complementary: both can be useful, depending on the problem at hand.

The proponents of the monetary approach have stressed the links between their re-formulation and the classical and neo-classical English economic literature.[1] One should not forget, however, that a number of Italian economists from the seventeenth until the early years of the present century had already analysed balance-of-payments and exchange-rate problems within the context of similar models and had arrived, in general, at the same conclusions. The first chapter of this book, therefore, is devoted to these Italian writers and to the similarity of their theories to the monetary approach. The purpose of the chapter is to revaluate the ideas of these economists, who are to a large extent neglected in modern literature – possibly because most of their work has not been translated into English. We shall see, for instance, that the wedge between income and expenditure occupies a central role in the analysis, by Carlo Beccaria (1754) and Pietro Verri (1772), of balance-of-payments fluctuations. The long-run neutrality of devaluation, too (Dornbusch, 1973b, 1974; Mundell, 1971), was clearly stated by Antonio Serra (1613) and, in this century, by Enrico Barone (1913).

The other chapters of the book contain empirical tests of various implications of the monetary approach on Italian post-war data. Chapter 2 tests the implications of the theory for the Italian balance of payments under fixed exchange rates (from 1951 to 1973). The methods used are twofold. In Section 2 the balance of payments is regressed directly on the main arguments of the demand and supply functions of money. The two-stage least-square method is used, in order to avoid reverse causation problems between the balance of payments and domestic assets of the Bank of Italy due to sterilisation policies. In Section 3 measures of *ex ante* flow excess demand for money are constructed for Italy and the rest of the world and then used to explain balance-of-payments fluctuations. The main conclusions to be drawn from the empirical tests are that the growth of productive capacity tended to improve the balance of payments, since it increased the demand for money; and that if this larger demand were not satisfied by monetary authorities through money creation, international reserves increased. However, as Italy is a very open economy, very dependent on imports of primary materials and investment goods, the short-run effect of income growth was negative. Furthermore, the increase of domestic assets of the Bank of Italy was fully compensated by reserve outflows; however, this did not imply the total loss of monetary independence because the compensation was not instantaneous. Finally, the depreciations of the effective exchange rate before 1973 had a positive impact on the balance of payments over an interval of a year because of the destruction of real monetary and financial assets which the depreciations generated. The tests of the Italian balance of payments are performed both on annual and quarterly data. The quarterly tests are performed separately for the first half of the 1960s and for the period from 1966 to 1973, when the effective exchange rate changed more often, and above all when the financing requirement of the Italian Treasury became much larger. The separate estimation of the balance of payments equation and the reaction function therefore give rise to quite interesting comparisons between the two periods.

Chapter 3 analyses in greater detail the objectives of Italian monetary policy and their evolution from 1960 to 1978. In order to clarify the constraint which increasing Treasury financing requirement imposed upon the Bank of Italy, the money supply process in Italy is analysed in Section 2, while in Section 3 the evolution of Italian bond markets after 1960 is sketched. Against the background of the institutional aspects it is easier to understand the type of monetary policy pursued by the Italian monetary authorities in the face of enlarged Treasury financing requirement after the mid-1960s, and to discuss the results of the tests of the reaction functions for three separate periods (1960–5, 1966–73 and 1974–8) presented in Section 4.

Chapter 4 contains empirical tests of the monetary approach to exchange-rate determination from February 1973 to December 1978. The dependent variable used in the tests is the percentage spread between the price of Italian banknotes in Zurich and the official exchange rate of the lira and Swiss franc. This spread is not subject to a time trend, as opposed to each of the two exchange rates mentioned above. In addition, it has the advantage of being sufficiently sensitive to changes in the underlying economic variables which affect the exchange rate, while the official exchange rate is not, also due to Bank of Italy interventions in the foreign exchange market. The use of the spread in the econometric tests gives rise to more robust conclusions, which are also valid for the more relevant official rate. The main hypothesis of the monetary approach is that for given real-money demands in the two areas considered, a monetary expansion leads in the final equilibrium position to a depreciation of the exchange rate of the same percentage. This hypothesis is fully confirmed by the empirical tests presented in Chapter 4. As far as the time lags are concerned, the tests indicate that relative monetary expansion exerted its full impact on the official exchange rate in about a year and a half. One section (Section 3) of this chapter is devoted to an analysis of the events leading to the 1976 exchange-rate crisis.

In Chapter 5 the overall balance of payments is split into its main components. The current and the capital accounts and the implications of the monetary approach for the current account are compared with those of the Cambridge view, which states that the current account is explained by the government budget deficit, independently of the way it is financed. The tests show that the government budget deficit matters only insofar as it leads to money creation. They also provide measures of the speed of adjustment of the current account, both under fixed and flexible exchange rates. Furthermore, they show that under fixed exchange rates the capital account reacted substantially faster to monetary disturbances than the current account, as one would expect, and that during the flexible exchange-rate period, the reaction pattern of the current account to monetary disturbances has increased somewhat.

All the empirical tests contained in this volume are reduced-form equations. It would certainly be useful to go beyond the test of these reduced-form equations and acquire information on the behaviour of the relevant markets. This, however, is outside the scope of this book.[2]

Despite the fact that the estimates presented are reduced forms they serve the useful purpose of demonstrating the relevance of developments in the money market, which other theories have neglected, for the balance of payments, the current and the capital accounts, and the exchange rate. They also imply that Italian monetary policy has been, under both systems of exchange rates, a powerful instrument to affect the level of economic activity in the very short run, but that within a year or so it has led inexorably to balance-of-payments and/or exchange-rate problems.

NOTES TO INTRODUCTION

1. See Johnson and Frenkel (1976), Chapter 1.
2. Small-scale structural models of the balance of payments which include all relevant markets and put particular emphasis on the speed of adjustment of actual to desired magnitudes have already been estimated for a number of countries including Australia (Jonson, 1978) and the United Kingdom (Knight and Wymer, 1979). For Italy, see Tullio (1980) and Chiesa (1979).

1 Aspects of Balance-of-Payments and Exchange-Rate Theory in Italian Economic Thought

INTRODUCTION

The objectives of this chapter are to discuss some aspects of the theory of balance-of-payments and exchange-rate changes which have dominated Italian economic thought throughout the last three and a half centuries, and to point out similarities of the Italian theory with the modern revival of the classical theory of the balance of payments and the exchange rate, commonly labelled as the 'monetary approach'. The chapter also clarifies some basic assumptions and fundamental implications of the theory upon which the empirical tests of the following chapters are based.

The field of analysis has been restricted in two important ways: (a) the period starts in 1613, when Antonio Serra's treatise *On the Reasons Why Countries, Where There Are No Mines, Abound in Gold and Silver* was first published in Naples[1], and ends in 1954 when *Corso di Economia Politica* by Bresciani-Turroni was published; (b) only the works of the major economists have been taken into consideration.

The monetary approach assumes the existence of a stable demand function for money and arbitrage across countries. Two fundamental implications following from these basic assumptions are: (a) the law of the natural distribution of money, and (b) the self-adjusting nature of balance-of-payments disequilibria. Although this theory has been largely developed under fixed exchange rates, this is not a necessary assumption. If exchange rates are perfectly flexible, the theory becomes a theory of exchange-rate changes, but the main implications of the monetary approach are not challenged.

Section 1 analyses the basic assumptions of the monetary approach and the two fundamental implications mentioned above. Related issues such as the idea that the proper framework within which balance-of-payments fluctuations and exchange-rate changes should be analysed is the money market, and the effects of monetary policy on the balance of payments and the exchange rate are also briefly discussed.

Section 2 analyses the importance Italian economists of the period under study attributed to the first basic assumption of the monetary approach: the existence of a stable demand function for money. Section 3 deals with the second basic assumption: the existence of arbitrage across countries. Section 4 deals with the law of the natural distribution of money, the stability of equilibrium, and the extent to which Italian economists considered the money market as the proper framework within which to analyse balance-of-payments and exchange-rate disturbances. Section 5 deals with the effect of monetary expansion on the balance of payments or on the exchange rate, if the latter is flexible. Finally, Section 6 is concerned with the interesting issue of whether Italian economists thought about adjustments of the balance of payments and the exchange rate to monetary disturbances more in terms of the direct-expenditure effect or of Hume's price-specie flow.[2] The monetary approach (Mundell, 1968, 1971; Johnson, 1973) has shifted its attention from Hume's price-specie flow to the direct-expenditure effect. The Italian forerunners of the monetary approach also seemed to rely more heavily on the direct-expenditure effect. This is probably because they had in mind very small economies with a relatively large foreign sector so that the scope for divergent price levels was small even in the short run. Only in the twentieth century, did Italian writers start to consider price effects as a mechanism of adjustment, but they did not take a clear-cut position for or against the price-specie flow. However, the two approaches are reconcilable. A mathematical appendix (Appendix 1.1) analyses the proposition of classical economics concerning the long-run effects of monetary policy on the level of foreign exchange reserves under different domestic and international monetary systems, disregarding the adjustment path to equilibrium, while in the other mathematical appendix (Appendix 1.2), a dynamic adjustment model of the balance of payments is developed with the aim of proving that the price-specie flow and the direct-expenditure effect are two extreme adjustment versions of the same basic classic model.

The sub-division adopted by topic is necessarily arbitrary since the arguments of the various sections are very closely linked. It follows that the decision to quote and discuss an author in one section instead of another was sometimes difficult. Section 7 contains concluding comments.

1. BASIC ASSUMPTIONS AND IMPLICATIONS OF THE MONETARY APPROACH

The basic assumptions of the monetary approach to balance-of-payments theory and the implications which follow from them will be outlined below.

Two crucial assumptions underlying the monetary approach are: (a) the existence of stable long-run demands for money in the countries whose balance of payments are analysed; and (b) the existence of arbitrage in goods markets, which tends to equate prices across countries and which is perfectly consistent with the belief that prices of goods (and price levels) diverge across countries even for long periods of time. Integrated capital markets are not essential for the conclusions of the monetary approach for they affect only the speed of adjustment to a disturbance (Swoboda, 1973).

From the above assumptions, a set of implications follows:

(1) A first implication is the law of the natural distribution of money, according to which the real quantity of money in any country cannot exceed the real quantity demanded in the long run. This holds both under fixed as well as flexible exchange rates. As shown in Section 4, the law was well known by Italian classical writers. Although they usually applied it to the world distribution of gold and silver, it can be extended to the post-war international monetary system (with fixed or flexible exchange rates).

Closely connected with the law of the natural distribution of money is the endogeneity of the money supply under fixed exchange rates. In a small open economy, which by assumption does not influence the world price level, not only the real quantity of money but also the nominal quantity is fixed. In the long run, an increase in nominal quantity of money generates an outflow of money through the balance of payments until the nominal quantity returns to its original level. However, over the short run, the central bank can keep the nominal quantity of money and the level of income above its long-run level (Prais, 1961). Over the long run the only effect of an expansionary monetary policy is therefore a substitution of reserves with domestic assets in the central bank's balance sheet (Mundell, 1968, 1971; Pareto, 1896). The implications of the monetary approach differ in the case of a large country. The loss of reserves will equal a fraction of the initial increase in the domestic assets of the central bank, and that fraction will be smaller the more the country can influence the world price level.[3]

(2) A second implication is the self-adjusting nature of balance-of-

payments or exchange-rate disequilibria. In a stationary economy in which the central bank does not try to pursue an independent monetary policy, all disequilibria will be self-adjusting. An increase in the world price of the key export goods is followed by a surplus in the balance of payments or the appreciation of the exchange rate, implying an undesired increase of real-money balances which will be eliminated through time until equilibrium is re-established. Alternatively, in the case of a reduction in the desired demand for money, the country will experience a balance-of-payments deficit or a depreciation of the exchange rate until the stock adjustment is accomplished.

(3) A third implication is that the proper framework within which to analyse the effects of a disturbance on the overall balance of payments or on the exchange rate is the money market. Under fixed exchange rates, according to Walras' law, the sum of the flow excess demands for goods and securities (a deficit in the overall balance of payments) must be equal to the flow-excess supply of money. Therefore, if one is not interested in subdividing the total payments imbalance into the capital and the trade account, it is simpler to concentrate on the money market. The same consideration applies to the flexible exchange rate case. Since a balance-of-payments or exchange-rate disequilibrium is always connected with a flow excess supply or demand for money and/or a stock adjustment in the money market, the balance-of-payments and exchange-rate changes are monetary phenomena.[4] This does not mean that the theory excludes the influence of real factors (Mussa, 1974). It only means that the effect on the balance of payments of non-monetary factors such as increase in a tariff or the growth of productivity should be analysed within the framework of the money market. Similarly, the theory does not rule out that a balance-of-payments surplus can be caused by the increase in the price of key export goods (Bresciani-Turroni, 1934, 1954).

Frequently, however, the forerunners of the monetary approach have associated, at least in Italian economic thought, payments and exchange-rate imbalances with over-expansions of the money supply.[5] This is probably because they had in mind countries with a relatively large foreign sector and with highly diversified imports, both by type and by origin, and exports, by type and by destination, so that as a result of the law of large numbers shocks on the flows and prices of single goods would tend to cancel each other out. On the other hand, proponents of the monetary approach have emphasised the real growth of economies (Mundell, 1968, 1971; Johnson, 1973). If the rate of growth of real income is high and the country's central bank does not fully monetise that growth by increasing sufficiently the domestic source component of the base, one would expect that country to have on average over the years a balance-of-payments surplus or an appreciating exchange rate. The experience of Japan, Germany and Italy during the 1950s and the 1960s fits this explanation.

There has been a continuing debate in recent years in Italy on the increasing Italian trade deficit in agricultural products. It is often argued that it is necessary to reduce the deficit in agricultural products as a first step towards reducing the overall trade deficit. Therefore, so the argument goes, capital should be invested in and labour attracted to agriculture. This position may be used to clarify how the monetary approach views the interactions between monetary and real variables in balance-of-payments analysis. According to the monetary approach, it is important to identify the sectors from which capital and labour would come. If labour were to be attracted from the pool of unemployed, national income would increase and the overall effect on the balance of payments would be positive. But if resources were to come from more productive sectors than agriculture, the net effect would be negative, because the overall productivity of labour, and hence national income and the demand for money, would be lower. However, if resources are attracted from less-productive sectors the net effect will be positive. It is probable that Italian agriculture is, or could be, a highly productive sector, but this is not guaranteed *a priori*. If it is not, the large agricultural trade gap is a sign of the increased international division of labour, and is to be welcomed. The main conclusion to be drawn is that by organising the analysis of how re-allocation of resources and real factors affect the balance of payments or the exchange rate around the money market, the risk of falling into partial-equilibrium analysis and of reaching wrong policy conclusions is considerably reduced.

In order to clarify further what is meant by the monetary nature of the balance of payments, we may consider briefly the effect of a devaluation of the currency. The domestic prices of imported and exported goods, and of goods which can be substituted for them, increase following a devaluation. The destruction of real-money balances induces people to hoard so as to re-establish their real-money holdings, and this, in turn, creates a wedge between income and expenditure which frees goods for export in exchange for the desired additions to the money stock. Thus, a surplus in the balance of payments is created, unless the central bank increases the domestic component of the base so as to satisfy all the excess demand for money generated by the devaluation. This analysis holds whether or not there are non-traded goods, whether or not other assets besides money are taken into account, whether the country is small or large, whether prices and wages are rigid or flexible, and finally whether the economy is growing or not.

(4) In discussing the endogeneity of the money stock under fixed exchange rates the related question of the effects of central bank policies on the balance of payments has already been implicitly raised. From the assumptions underlying the monetary approach, it is possible to make forecasts concerning the impact of various policies on the balance of payments: the replacement of full-bodied commodity money with paper money will induce gold and silver to flow out of the country; the substitution of bank deposits for paper money will reduce the stock of gold and silver in the country (Hume, 1752). In the same way, the effects of other policy measures on the exchange rate can be traced.

Section 5 discusses in detail the effect of the debasement[6] of a currency in a small-scale European economy of the sixteenth to the eighteenth centuries and the connection between the debasement of a currency and Gresham's Law. It deals, too, with the marked similarity, as far as their effect on the balance of payments is concerned, between the debasement of a currency at that time and an increase in the domestic source component of the monetary base in today's institutional framework of developed countries.

(5) It does not follow from assumptions 1 and 2 that the adjustment to monetary disturbances originating within a small country has to be exclusively direct, in the sense that during the adjustment process the domestic price level cannot increase above the world price level. Both the price-specie flow and the direct-expenditure effect are consistent with the monetary approach. The adjustment lies somewhere in between, even in the absence of non-traded goods.[7] Favouring one extreme over another means making an empirical judgment as to how quickly arbitrage operates, as to the ratio of traded to non-traded goods in the economy and the degree of capital mobility. The monetary approach, as developed in recent years, has relied heavily upon the direct-expenditure effect. This can be justified on the grounds of: (a) increased simplicity of model building; (b) an empirical judgment that markets are indeed very deeply interconnected and arbitrage operates very rapidly, and that the ratio of traded to non-traded goods as well as capital mobility is high; (c) the emphasis of the monetary approach on the wedge between income and expenditure (hoarding) as the central mechanism of adjustment (Frenkel, 1974); and (d) the emphasis of the existing monetary approach literature on long-run propositions and the relative neglect until recently of the dynamics of adjustment.

On the other hand, since the publication of Hume's *On the Balance of*

Trade the price-specie-flow version seems to have dominated English economic thought. However, as stated in the introduction, early Italian writers all seemed to rely more heavily on the direct-expenditure effect and during this century they have not taken a clear-cut position in favour of one or the other. In Appendix 1.2 both versions of the adjustment process will be derived as two extreme cases from a highly simplified monetary model.

2. THE EXISTENCE OF AN IMPLICIT OR EXPLICIT LONG-RUN DEMAND FOR MONEY[8]

The assumptions underlying the monetary approach to balance-of-payments theory, together with their implications, have been briefly set out in Section 1. This and the succeeding sections analyse how these assumptions and implications were emphasised by Italian economists.

The role of the demand for money in the analysis of exchange-rate changes can be traced in the work of Antonio Serra, although he did not refer explicitly to a function. Serra's short treatise *On the Reason Why Countries, Where There Are No Mines, Abound in Gold and Silver* (published in Naples in 1613) is divided into three parts: the first chapter is concerned with the factors that determine the abundance of commodities, the second chapter deals with a theory of the effects of the devaluation of a small open economy's currency, and the third chapter analyses the problem of how a government can increase the amount of gold and silver in the country. 'The reasons why countries abound in gold and silver' were the ones which determine the abundance of commodities in the economy, namely abundance of 'goods' (by which Serra means the level of agricultural production), a geographical position favourable to trade (Serra contrasts Venice with Naples in this respect), the level of industry and craft production, and – a closely connected factor – the 'quality' of the people, that is, their skill, industriousness and entrepreneurial capacity. A final factor was the type of policy pursued by the government and whether or not it encouraged commerce, industry and economic activity. The aim of the book was to show that the proposal to devalue the currency in order to solve the kingdom's balance-of-payments problems would have been ineffective. He argues that 'the level of the exchange rate[9] does not influence at all the inflow of money through the export of goods' (Serra, 1613, p. 97), thus establishing the long-run neutrality of devaluation (Mundell, 1971, Dornbusch, 1973b, 1974). Although Serra did not explicitly introduce a demand function for money, his first chapter can be considered as a complete theory of the demand for money (or, more precisely, of the demand for gold and silver), both from the logical sequence of the chapters and the aim of the book. A government could solve its balance-of-payments problems only by promoting a high demand for gold and silver by the economy. A devaluation did not change the demand and was therefore ineffective, and so were exchange controls: 'The simple prohibition of the export of money does not represent a real measure and is of no help in making countries abound in gold and silver; on the contrary, it is rather damaging' (Serra, 1613, p. 132).

After Serra's treatise it is impossible to find in Italian economic thought until the first half of the nineteenth century a treatment of the balance of payments or of the exchange rate that is so thoroughly based on an implicit or explicit theory of the demand for money. However, statements relating arguments of a non-specified demand function for money to the balance of payments are to be found in a number of writers. Ferdinando Galiani, for instance, writes:

> The one who says that in order to avoid the outflow of money, one must establish good laws, build hospitals, organise good armies, create cautious judges, and cultivate industriously the land, would mention the true and certain remedy to the extraction (Galiani, 1750, Vol. 11, p. 191);

and elsewhere:

> when industry develops in a country, the latter becomes more a creditor than a debtor with respect to neighbouring countries; hence, after being provided with the goods of the others, it will still draw money because of the surplus [in her balance of payments] (Galiani, 1750, Vol. 10, p. 176).

Beccaria, in discussing the lack of data on foreign trade, points out that the following circumstances indicate 'active trade' (a surplus in the trade balance): (1) population grows, (2) agriculture develops both in intensity and extension, (3) interest rates on loans fall, and (4) prices rise (Beccaria, 1754, p. 93).

The monetary approach obtains the above results from the small-country assumption: if interest rates fall, the balance of payments improves and if the price level goes up, the balance of payments also improves (Johnson, 1973).

Gian Rinaldo Carli argues that the discovery of America reduced the level of economic activity in Italy because trade with the Orient became less important. 'We have to conclude (he wrote) that Italy has also been greatly impoverished, and that therefore precious metals have become rare and dear' (Carli, 1760, Vol. 20, p. 325).

In the first half of the nineteenth century, Carlo Cattareo analysed world inflation after the discovery of America within the framework of an explicit demand and supply of world money, the stock demand and supply of world money being the sums of the national demands and supplies.[10] The main arguments of his demand functions were population, the degree of the division of labour, wealth, and the extent to which precious metals wear out. Sometimes he also considered the distribution of wealth as an argument.

In discussing the value of paper currency, he writes:

> . . . its value comes from demand and demand from the need for it, . . . national paper currency will therefore not be exempt from the supreme laws of supply and demand and from the danger of depreciation and refusal (Cattaneo, 1839, Vol. 2, p. 279).

Cattaneo also distinguishes between stocks and flows, when he compares the fluctuations of the relative price of gold in terms of silver in ancient times with its fluctuations in modern times:

> The least commerce was widespread and the smaller the stock of precious metals, the more sudden were changes in their relative prices, and a small inflow of one or the other was enough to change them. Nowadays, the immensity of the stock of metals hoarded in so many centuries of human history and the speed of trade flows make any sudden disequilibrium of values impossible. The revolution of Spanish America which reduced to one third the output of the mines there, did not cause any direct fluctuation in the value of metals (Cattaneo, 1839, Vol. 2, pp. 204-5).

Later in the nineteenth century Vilfredo Pareto, after describing the effects on the balance of payments of increasing by an amount T the supply of paper currency in circulation, concluded: 'We would observe exactly the same phenomena if for a given quantity of T, other things would change and increase the demand for the capital money-in-circulation' (Pareto, 1896, p. 360).

3. ARBITRAGE AND THE LAW OF ONE PRICE

The second assumption underlying the monetary approach, namely the existence of arbitrage, is treated at length by Italian economists, particularly Montanari, Barone and Bresciani-Turroni.

Montanari writes about the law of one price and the forces which bring it about:

> . . . through commerce the price of things in all places becomes so regulated that one finds no more difference [in prices], than can be explained by transport costs, risk of travel, tariffs, and other things. . . . Since if, once account is taken of these expenses, the price of oil were still much cheaper in Abruzzo[11] than in Venice, merchants would transport so much more to make profits, that less being left over in Abruzzo the price would rise there, and more being found in Venice the price would fall there. I remember having used several times in this connection and with a gain in clarity, the analogy of liquids, since it seems to me that the prices of goods in the world equalize themselves through trade in the same way as stagnant waters do (Montanari, 1680, pp. 51–3).

Elsewhere he discusses the effect of the opening-up of trade with America and emphasises the profit motive behind arbitrage:

> The inflow of gold had the effect of making all the products of Europe more rare than before and of causing prices to fluctuate for a long time; but now they have levelled off in such a way that it is no longer possible for those who trade with America to become rich in such a short time as it was before (Montanari, 1680, p. 55).

Arbitrage was considered as a flow of goods, but more often the same idea was expressed directly in terms of flows of money. Broggia, for instance, wrote:

> By nature anything flows to where it is well paid compared with other places. The value of money is in general the things that one can buy and sell in exchange for money; and where the value of one money . . . is such that for the same amount of metal you can buy more things than elsewhere . . . , there the metal and money abound (Broggia, 1743, Vol. 4, p. 337).

Similarly, Beccaria:

> Those who have money will seek to spend it where it is valued higher . . . i.e., where it obtains more things than where it is valued less . . . therefore for the same quantity of goods nations with less money will be preferred to nations with more money (Beccaria, 1754, pp. 84–5).

Among Italian economists, arbitrage and the law of one price were emphasised by Pantaleoni, Barone, Pareto, and Bresciani-Turroni. Pantaleoni stated:

> We will observe a flow of money towards the market where prices are low from the market where prices are high, until the larger quantity of money in the former . . . and the smaller quantity of money in the latter . . . has established a level of prices common to both markets. (Pantaleoni, 1894, pp. 267–77).

Barone explicitly used the small-country assumption, and discussed arbitrage in the context of that assumption:

> The movements of prices originating from monetary disturbances are limited both by the difficulty that prices have to move all together . . . and, above all, by the competition of other markets through the mechanism of international trade. We must add that, at least for some of the most widely consumed products, there are international prices that the producer's and consumer's markets determine jointly . . . but that a single market cannot influence very much, unless it is the most powerful producer or the largest consumer . . . (Barone, 1913, p. 146).

Arbitrage brings about equality of prices for the same goods and equality of price levels. It is also the force which brings about the natural distribution of money and renders the equilibrium thus established a stable one. Most Italian writers were well aware of these effects, as will be seen in the next section.

4. THE LAW OF THE NATURAL DISTRIBUTION OF MONEY AND THE STABILITY OF EQUILIBRIUM

The law of the natural distribution of money was implicitly referred to by Italian economists, sometimes through an analogy with interconnected volumes of water, the water being the analogue of money and the level of the water being the world price level:

> Therefore, in the same way as when stagnant water that before was lying at a perfect level . . . is connected by a canal to another body of stagnant water that is farther away, we see for *some times* [my italics] uncommon movements in the one and in the other, until the surplus of water that was in the one is transfused into the other and a new level is established that is common to both (Montanari, 1680, pp. 293–4).

Here, Montanari considers the opening-up of trade as a necessary condition for the natural distribution of money to come about. He also makes an analytical distinction between the path of adjustment and the final equilibrium position. Galiani, after making the same distinction, goes one step further by stating the principle of the stability of equilibrium:

> First, one should not consider at all the first movements of things but only the permanent and fixed states, and by doing so order and equality are always found. . . . Second, no shock can occur in nature that carries things to an infinite end; a certain moral gravity that is in everything will keep them away from the infinite straight line and will make them turn in an everlasting but finite circle. What I have said I will apply a *hundred times to money;* readers should be convinced that *the laws of commerce correspond with great exactness to the laws of gravity and of fluids and nothing else* [my italics] (Galiani, 1750, Vol.10, p. 91).

Italian economists of the end of the nineteenth century and the beginning of the twentieth stated their belief in the stability of equilibrium in less picturesque but more precise terms than Galiani, and were also more explicit in linking it to the natural distribution of money. Barone, for instance, wrote that 'under the action of free competition the gold in existence and the gold produced in the mines are distributed among the different countries. . . . ' (Barone, 1913, pp. 139–40). The equilibrium thus established is, according to Barone, a stable equilibrium. He continues: 'The equilibrium that is established is a stable equilibrium: in the sense that if it is disturbed, forces develop which tend to bring it back to the original position' (Barone, 1913, p. 140). Pareto expressed his ideas on the natural distribution of money and the stability of equilibrium in almost precisely the same terms

(Pareto, 1896, p. 341). Basically the same idea is found also in Bresciani-Turroni who praised the classics for having provided this useful insight (Bresciani-Turroni, 1954, p. 165).

Closely linked to the stability of equilibrium is the self-adjusting nature of balance-of-payments disequilibria. In fact, they are two aspects of the same thing. Serra, to put it in Schumpter's words, 'saw much of it' (Schumpter, 1954, p. 365). Beccaria also saw clearly the temporary nature of balance-of-payments disequilibria and their relationship to stock-adjustment phenomena:

> . . . not over a long period, nor continuously, but only for a limited time, can the value of purchases exceed the value of sales, because not all the money that exists in a nation is in circulation. The money that lies dead and inactive in the hands of the public, can for some time make up for the excess of payments over sales, . . . but once that money is exhausted, the possibility of buying more than is sold must vanish, indeed [even] the quantity of the one which is in circulation will decrease. . . . But at the same time as the quantity of money goes down, prices go down . . . and that way the impoverished nation will start again to increase its revenues and to return to equilibrium with more frequent sales (Beccaria, 1754, p. 87).

This could be seen as incorporating a consumption function of the form originally introduced by Prais[12], since the excess of expenditure over income is related to the excess of the actual stock of money over the quantity needed for transaction purposes and the quantity held 'inactive and dead'. Verri, on the other hand, saw the balance-of-payments disequilibrium and the excess of expenditure over income as related to the change in the stock of all assets ('capital'):

> The country in which yearly consumption has been higher than annual production has reduced its wealth, and one can say of it what one says of a family, when besides its annual rent [income], it spends part of its capital (Verri, 1772, p. 179).

It was the recognition of the central role of assets in balance-of-payments analysis that led the classical Italian writers to infer that balance-of-payments surpluses and deficits are self-adjusting and not repeating. Verri, for instance, wrote that 'the value of all imported commodities must necessarily be equal to the value of all exported commodities after a certain period of time' (Verri, 1772, p. 176).

Johnson (1976) maintains that the crucial difference between the monetary approach and alternative theories is the self-adjusting nature of balance-of-payments disequilibria, and the evidence reported in this section shows that Italian balance-of-payments theory shares this characteristic with the monetary approach.

The analysis of this and the previous sections show how often in Italian economic thought the analysis of balance-of-payments disturbances centred on the money market and how crucial the role assigned to assets (money) was. The idea that the balance of payments is a safety valve for an excess demand or supply of money was expressed by Beccaria:

> Therefore it is possible to understand how important the increase and the maintenance of foreign trade is, not only for the useful increase of the money that flows into the country, but also for the no less useful and sometimes essential outflow of money (Beccaria, 1954, p. 85).

When quoting writers prior to the nineteenth century the terms 'balance of payments' and 'balance of trade' have been used (and will continue to be used) interchangeably, since it can be safely assumed that capital movements were at the time either non-existent or not very relevant to the countries concerned. As capital movements grow in importance changes in the stock of money can no longer be related to the balance of trade but must be related to the overall balance of payments. Barone, after discussing this issue in detail (Barone, 1913, pp. 154–6) concluded that 'the money that is exported or imported is not at all the difference between imports and exports' (Barone, 1913, p. 157). On the other hand, Verri was arguing almost 150 years earlier that 'the difference that results between imports and exports is considered to be the stock of money that must have risen or fallen in the state' (Verri, 1772, p. 178).

5. THE EFFECTS OF MONETARY POLICY ON THE BALANCE OF PAYMENTS AND THE EXCHANGE RATE, AND THE NEUTRALITY OF DEVALUATION

In considering the effects of monetary policy on the balance of payments and the exchange rate, changes in monetary systems from the seventeenth century until the present day must be taken into account; but once the differences in institutional arrangements are allowed, the conclusions reached by the various authors as to the effects of monetary policy are practically the same. The effects of expansionary monetary policy and of devaluation of the exchange rate are described below in the context of a national and international gold and/or silver standard, and compared with the effects in a modern institutional setting. This is followed by an account of the effects of an expansionary monetary policy where baser metals are used to supplement gold and /or silver coinage.

In the context of a national and international gold and/or silver standard, it can safely be assumed that foreign exchange dealers become aware much sooner than the public at large that the silver or gold content of a currency has altered. Since in this case the relative price of currencies is determined by their respective metal content, the following statement can be made about the speed adjustment of prices when a silver or gold currency is debased:

> . . . and if this change [the debasement] occurred in an island separated from any trade with foreigners, the old ideas[13] would change very slowly. The existence of trade, however, means that the first to change is the exchange rate, the thermometer of countries; if it did not change one country would absorb the other country's money (Galiani, 1750, Vol. 11, p. 85).

Galiani implicitly distinguished a pegged from an unpegged exchange rate. In the latter case, the debasement would be analogous to a modern Western economy, with perfectly flexible exchange rates, increasing the domestic component of the base.

As far as the ineffectiveness of a devaluation is concerned, Serra's belief in the neutrality of devaluation has been already mentioned in Section 2.[14] However, there is an important difference between a devaluation in Serra's day and a devaluation of a paper currency in the institutional setting of modern monetary systems: Serra's neutrality was a short-run as well as long-run neutrality, while a devaluation in a modern context would be neutral only in the long run, since the balance of payments will be in surplus during the adjustment process.[15] As in Serra's day, however, the final real quantity of money in the economy will be the same as before. The difference of the short-run effects on the balance of payments depends on the different nature of money in the two systems (full-bodied commodity money in Serra and Galiani as opposed to fiat money in today's context).

Barone, who already had a modern paper currency system in mind, pointed out that the positive effects are temporary and warned against considering them as permanent, thus emphasising the long-run neutrality of a devaluation:

> To believe that a depreciated currency can increase exports and decrease imports is a very common error. The error stems from considering as permanent what is an immediate and transitory effect – limited to some products only – in the adjustment from one equilibrium to the other (Barone, 1913, p. 144).

If we now turn to a comparison of the effects of the debasement of a less-noble metal coin with the effect of an increase in the domestic component of the monetary base in today's institutional framework, we may begin by assuming that the less-noble metal coin is pegged in terms of gold and silver and that it is not accepted internationally; similarly, that in today's institutional framework the exchange rate is fixed. The monetary approach concludes that the longer-run effect of monetary policy is the loss of foreign exchange reserves (Mundell, 1968; Johnson, 1973).[16]

If a copper currency is debased, gold and silver in circulation start flowing out of the country;[17] since gold and silver are foreign exchange reserves held by private citizens, the conclusion of the monetary aoproach holds. With foreign exchange reserves in private hands, the observed law is an application of Gresham's Law.[18]

Montanari describes the effects of the raising of the currency in Poland as follows:

> . . . those who had to bring money out of Poland were looking for old talers . . . almost all of which were already outside the kingdom; furthermore, the few that were still in the country were valued at a much higher price than the original ones, and that way the good coins increased [in price] to such an extent that . . . (Montanari, 1680, p. 169).

At first the country loses gold and silver but finally the pegging has to be given up.

Broggia argued that since a kilogram of copper in the kingdom of Naples is worth a kilogram of copper in Rome, if a copper currency is debased while the government pegs the gold and silver price of copper, gold and silver will flow out of the country (Broggia, 1743, p. 366); if the pegging is stopped then all prices will go up either immediately or with a lag (p. 380). He added that 'in order to stop the export of money . . . there is no better remedy than to give to the currency the right value, suitable to the metal' (p. 366).

Carli considered explicitly the size and openness of the country in relation to the effect of the debasement of a currency and concluded that the effects were much more devastating for a small than for a large country:

> . . . the circumstances of the Romans [at the time of the First Punic War] discharge them sufficiently, since they were isolated from any foreign trade (Carli, 1754, p. 109).
>
> But when the Empire collapsed and the peoples were divided and Europe was split up into a large number of republics and kingdoms and Italy into an even greater number, the abritrariness of monies ceased, for it could not [the arbitrariness] continue without causing its [the money's] collapse, since among the separate countries trade was established by necessity of interest, and one nation became dependent on another (Carli, 1754, p. 115).

Implicitly Carli expressed here the idea of the endogeneity of the nominal stock of money for a small open country with fixed exchange rates and the exogeneity of a large or closed one, i.e., the independence of monetary policy only for large or closed countries.

He also was aware of the fact that if a country debased its currency when the rest of the world was debasing its own, the disruption would be less severe:

> But why did France not lose its money after so many successive alterations? Because the quantity of gold and silver which from time to time arrived there [in France] from India and America has supported it [France] in such a way that the evil has not reached the point which it would undoubtedly have reached otherwise (Carli, 1754, p. 156).

As stated above, the effects of the debasement of the currency can be described as an application of Gresham's Law, and this is true whatever the stage of development of the domestic monetary system, provided gold or silver coins still circulate. At the end of the nineteenth century Pantaleoni was describing these effects as follows:

> In the case in which, alongside a metallic currency a paper currency with fixed exchange rates also circulates, if the paper currency

> becomes over-abundant it will drive out [of circulation] the metallic currency, because partly it will be hoarded and partly it will be used for international payments in which foreign currencies are accepted on the basis of their metallic content . . . . (Pantaleoni, 1894, p. 267);

and similarly Pareto:

> Gresham's law is a corollary of the more general theorem which we have proved on the stability of economic equilibrium. Since it is not possible to increase the quantity of money which corresponds to that equilibrium, if we add a given quantity of money then necessarily part of the stock of money emigrates or is demonetised (Pareto, 1896, p. 413)

Pareto's world was of a mixed gold and paper currency type. The disturbance he considered was an injection of paper currency of amount *T*. He described the final effect as follows: 'The stock of money will go back to its original level, but in the circulation a given quantity of currency *T* will have been substituted for gold' (Pareto, 1896, p. 360).

Pareto, who based his analysis explicitly on the demand for money, came therefore to the same conclusion as Mundell (1968): an expansionary monetary policy leads to a substitution of domestic assets for international reserves in the central bank's balance sheet.

It is easy to see from the issues discussed, that most of the Italian economists under study were well aware that the cause of balance-of-payments or exchange-rate difficulties was very often an excess of government expenditure over revenues, financed by money creation. Serra was aware of it and, similarly, Carli argued that 'in addition it often happens that princes inveigh against the effects and not the causes and once the latter are removed the former also disappear' (Carli, 1754, p. 185).

In the twentieth century an author who has devoted particular attention to the effects of high government budget deficits is Bresciani-Turroni, who analysed the monetary disorders in Germany after World War I as follows: 'During the months following the end of the war, the government budget deficit remained the primary cause of the increase in issues [of paper money] and of the devaluation of the exchange rate' (Bresciani-Turroni, 1924, p. 19).[19] He maintained that the chain of causation could not run from the devaluation of the exchange rate to the budget deficit because it was evident that 'a discrepancy between demand and supply of foreign exchange cannot cause a *continuous* fall of the exchange rate unless it is accompanied by a *continuous* [my italics] increase in issues of paper money' (Bresciani-Turroni, 1924, p. 46). Furthermore, it was clear in his mind that the effects follow the cause with a lag:

> But it is important not to forget that the last stage of the depreciation of the mark was, to a large extent, the direct consequence of an erroneous financial policy during the preceding years (Bresciani-Turroni, 1924, p. 53).

6. THE DIRECT-EXPENDITURE EFFECT VERSUS THE PRICE-SPECIE FLOW

As stated in Section 1, the monetary approach as recently developed relies heavily on the direct-expenditure effect, while the price-specie flow seems to have dominated English economic thought. However, Italian economists have placed a great deal of emphasis on the direct-expenditure effect. This is particularly true of early Italian writers, as we shall see in this section, and may be due to the fact that Italy was split into many very small and extremely open countries.

In very small and open countries, which are well connected by sea and by land, arbitrage is likely to operate very fast and the non-traded goods sector is likely to be relatively small. Hence, there is very little scope for divergence of the domestic price level from the foreign one.

Mentions of gold and silver flowing out of the country following a domestic disturbance, without reference to prior price level changes, are very common and several are quoted in the previous section.[20]

The direct-expenditure effect was also clearly expressed by Galiani:[21]

> India, where silver was lacking, *soon absorbed the over-abundant* quantity which was lying in Europe; therefore the value of metals *did not change in proportion with the quantity which had come from America*, but much less so . . . . (Galiani, 1750, Vol. 10, p. 46).

Later he clarified this concept:

> America sends the metals to us . . . some are employed to increase the stock of money and therefore its value tends to decrease, *although imperceptibly*; much we keep in tools *and the rest is sent to India* (Galiani, 1750, p. 47).

Cattaneo argued that the likelihood of fluctuations of the price of silver, with respect to gold, is small when the stock of precious metals accumulated from the past is large, and 'the speed of trade flows' is high. He thought that in the nineteenth century the gold price of silver was largely determined in world markets. Hence, a large reduction of the world output of either gold or silver would hardly affect their relative price in the country or area where the precious metals were produced, nor elsewhere (Cattaneo, 1839, pp. 203–4), which amounts to adhering to the direct-expenditure effect.[22]

Pareto also considered the direct-expenditure effect as the relevant mechanism of adjustment:

> If the quantity of money is increased in a closed economy, the excess disappears into industrial uses. If it is increased in an open economy a small quantity still goes into industrial uses, but most of it emigrates abroad (Pareto, 1896, p. 346).

In the twentieth century, Bresciani-Turroni considered at some length the issue of the direct-expenditure effect versus the price-specie flow. In writing about Egypt's balance of payments, he stated:

> Contrary to what happens according to the classical scheme [the price-specie flow], in the case of Egypt the *changes in purchasing power* of the Egyptian population exert an overwhelming and almost immediate effect (Bresciani-Turroni, 1954, p. 207).

He further argued that imports increased, with a lag of about one year, because of the increase in Egypt's purchasing power. Egyptian prices did not increase at all, or if they did, they exerted only a marginal effect on exports, because Egypt exported cotton and onions, the prices for which were determined in world markets.

On the other hand, as far as the devaluation of the mark after World War I is concerned, Bresciani-Turroni did not take a clear-cut position in favour of or against the price-specie flow:

> The new paper money issued was increasing continuously the price level, and the equilibrium level of the exchange rate was changing according to the fall in the 'internal' value [of the currency]. Or the new money by flowing directly to the foreign exchange market was depressing the external value of the mark first and was causing an increase in prices afterwards (Bresciani-Turroni, 1924, p.72).

With respect to the issue of the direct-expenditure effect versus the price-specie flow, Genovesi stood out as an exception, since he emphasised particularly the price-specie flow:

> If money grows out of all proportion in only one country in Europe . . . it ruins trade . . . because it makes manufactures *very expensive* [my italics] with respect to those of other countries (Genovesi, 1765a, p.65).

Elsewhere he took the extreme view that prices increase in the same proportion as the quantity of money during the adjustment process (Genovesi, 1765b, p.295). It should be noted, however, that he refers quite often to Hume in his descriptions of the adjustment process.

It should be noted, too, that the issue of the direct-expenditure effect versus the price-specie flow discussed in this section bears a close resemblance to the famous dispute between Keynes and Ohlin over German reparations. The dispute centred upon whether changes in the terms of trade (which in a one-sector model of each country are equal to relative price level changes) are necessary in order to achieve equilibrium in the balance of payments. Ohlin, being more Keynesian than Keynes himself, argued that income changes would be sufficient to bring about the real transfer, thus adhering to the direct-expenditure effect, while Keynes thought that relative price level changes would be necessary.

7. CONCLUSIONS

The previous sections show how the assumptions and implications of the monetary approach were already familiar to most of the Italian classical writers, although not all of them proposed a reasonably comprehensive general equilibrium theory of the balance of payments. Among those who did, Serra, Pareto and Barone at least should be mentioned.

As far as the underlying assumptions of the monetary approach are concerned, arbitrage was emphasised by several writers, but an explicit reference to a demand for money is found only in Cattaneo and Pareto. This is one difference between the Italian classical tradition and the monetary approach. The difference is not crucial, however, since there is implicit in the writings of Italian economists a non-specified demand function for money, generally of a transaction type,[23] which allows them to assume most of the basic implictions of the monetary approach:

the self-adjusting nature of balance-of-payments disequilibria and the related distinction between the long run and the short run, the neutrality of devaluation, and the effects of monetary policy on the balance of payments and the exchange rate. In addition, Beccaria and Verri can be credited with the insight that balance-of-payments disequilibria necessarily imply a wedge between income and expenditure.

Besides introducing explicitly the concept of the demand for money, the monetary approach represents, in several important respects, a step forward with respect to the balance-of-payments theory which dominated Italian economic thought. It has stated more clearly assumptions and implications in the context of precise general-equilibrium models of the economy; it has shown that the basic conclusions retain their validity in the context of a variety of different models; it has made a considerable effort to integrate international monetary theory into the real theory of trade which has in the meantime developed; and more recently it has devoted more attention to the adjustment path of the system to the new equilibrium position after a disturbance. Finally, the availability of modern econometric techniques has allowed several implications of the theory to be tested, although simple graphical techniques have sometimes proved equally useful in verifying some implications of the theory.[24]

The most interesting feature of Italian classical balance-of-payments theory is its reliance on the direct-expenditure effect as opposed to the price-specie flow which seems to have been more common in English balance-of-payments theory. The explanation advanced in this chapter is that Italy was divided into a number of small states, with good communications by sea and by land, and with arbitrage operating very fast.

The monetary approach has been laregely developed by non-Americans, who have relied heavily on the small-country assumption, both because it greatly simplifies analysis and because it comes close to depicting their countries' real situation.

Whatever the reasons which led Italian economists and the monetary approach to emphasise the direct-expenditure effect as opposed to the price-specie flow, Appendix 1.2 shows that both are compatible with the basic classical model of the balance of payments, the relative importance of the one versus the other during the adjustment process depending on such factors as the degree of capital mobility, the ratio of traded to non-traded goods and how fast arbitrage operates to equate the prices of the same goods across countries.

APPENDIX 1.1: THE LONG-RUN EFFECT OF MONETARY POLICY ON THE LEVEL OF FOREIGN EXCHANGE RESERVES

The purpose of this appendix is to formalise and clarify some of the propositions discussed in Section 5 of this chapter. The long-run effect of changes in the domestic source component of the monetary base on the level of foreign exchange reserves under fixed exchange rates depends on the 'size' of the country. If its 'size' approaches zero the nominal quantity of money is totally endogenous. We shall consider a two-country world and prove the above statement in the context of a simple monetary model. Let D stand for the domestic component of the base, R for the foreign component, P for the price level, r for the interest rate, y for the level of real income, L for the real quantity of money demanded and $\overline{R}$ for the level of world reserves. We assume that the demand function for money is homogeneous of degree one in prices and that the level of real income is exogenously determined.[25]

Case 1: International gold exchange standard; domestic fiat monies
Let the exchange rate be fixed and for simplicity be equal to one. We shall assume also 100 percent reserve requirements. In addition arbitrage establishes a unique world price level in the long run. Let the domestic country be a non-reserve-currency country. An asterisk represents foreign variables.

$$D + R = PL(r, y) \tag{A.1}$$

$$D^* + R^* = P^* L^*(r^*, y^*) \tag{A.2}$$

$$P = P^* \tag{A.3}$$

and

$$r = r^* \tag{A.4}$$

because of perfect capital movements. By definition

$$R + R^* = \overline{R}. \tag{A.5}$$

Differentiating totally (A.1) and (A.2) and taking into account (A.3), (A.4) and (A.5) and solving for dR we get:

(A.6) $$\mathrm{d}R = \frac{L^*}{L+L^*}\mathrm{d}D = -\frac{1}{\alpha+1}\mathrm{d}D$$

Let us call $\alpha = L/L^*$ the effective size of the country. If α approaches zero, the country loses practically an amount $\mathrm{d}D$ of reserves. The larger α, the smaller the reserve loss for a given change in D. Notice that $\mathrm{d}R$ is also the definition of the balance of payments. See Chapters 3 and 4, where regressions of $\mathrm{d}R$ on $\mathrm{d}D$ and other variables are presented for Italy.

Now consider the case of a reserve-currency country (for instance, the United States). Variables marked with an asterisk refer now to the rest of the world with respect to the reserve-currency country. G represents the US gold stock and R_S^* dollar reserves of the rest of the world.

(A.1′) $$D+G = PL(r, y)$$

(A.2′) $$D^*+G^*+R_S^* = P^*L^*(r^*, y^*)$$

(A.3) and (A.4) remain unchanged.

(A.5′) $$\overline{R} = G+G^*+R_S^*$$

(A.6′) $$G+G^* = \overline{G}.$$

Let us define the fraction $\lambda = \mathrm{d}R_S^*/\mathrm{d}G^*$ which represents the desired (or imposed) composition of additions to its reserves by the rest of the world. We want to know how much gold the reserve-currency country loses if it increases D. By solving the system (A.1′)–(A.6′) we get:

(A.7) $$\mathrm{d}G = -\mathrm{d}D\left[\frac{1}{1+\alpha(1+\lambda)}\right].$$

The effective size of the US is measured by $\alpha(1+\lambda)$; it is increased by a factor $(1+\lambda)$ with respect to the case in which it was not a reserve-currency country. Given α, if the rest of the world does not accept dollars, i.e., $\lambda = 0$, the formula (A.7) reduces to that obtained for a non-reserve-currency country. At the other extreme, if the world is on a dollar standard $\lambda = +\infty$ and $\mathrm{d}G = 0$.

For the reserve-currency country the definition of the balance of payments is:

$$B = \mathrm{d}G - \mathrm{d}R_S^* = \mathrm{d}G(1+\lambda).$$

Using (A.7) we get:

$$B = -\mathrm{d}D\left[\frac{1}{1/(1+\lambda)+\alpha}\right].$$

For regression of the US balance of payments on dD and other variables see Tullio (1979a). When λ tends to infinity and α is about 1, the expected coefficient of dD is about -1. With $\lambda = 0$, the coefficient would be $-1/2$.

Case 2: Pure domestic and international gold standard

(A.1″) $$R = PL(r, y)$$

(A.2″) $$R^* = P^*L^*(r^*, y^*).$$

(A.3), (A.4) and (A.5) remain as before and R stands now for gold reserves. Assume a gold discovery in the country (an increase in $\overline{R}$), differentiate as before and solve for dR. We get:

$$\mathrm{d}R = -\mathrm{d}R^* = -\frac{1}{1+\alpha}\mathrm{d}\overline{R}.$$

Again if α approaches zero the country loses almost all of the gold that has been discovered. The gold discovery can be huge and the world price level can be very much affected, but the country will keep only a fraction $(1 - 1/(1+\alpha))$ of the gold discovered. This is nothing but the law of the natural distribution of money in its older formulation relating to a commodity-money world. The definition of the balance of payments for the country in question is dR.

APPENDIX 1.2: THE DIRECT-EXPENDITURE EFFECT VERSUS THE PRICE-SPECIE FLOW

As pointed out in this chapter, the direct-expenditure effect and the price-specie flow are not inconsistent with each other in a short-run dynamic model. The stock-excess supply of money, in the country which increases the domestic source component of the base, exerts its influence both on the domestic price level and directly on the balance of payments. At the same time the ensuing difference between the domestic and the world price level also influences the balance of payments. We have, therefore, a direct effect on the balance of payments and an indirect one (working through relative price level changes), operating jointly. I assume a two-country world and that real income is determined exogenously also in short-run disequilibrium. In this respect the model is a partial-equilibrium one, since the changes in the real sector, and in particular the changes brought about by monetary policy, are assumed away for simplicity.

Throughout the period of adjustment to the disturbance the long-run demand for money function is considered as relatively insensitive to changes in the real interest rate and the expected rate of inflation. Dots indicate time derivatives, variables relating to foreign countries are marked with an asterisk. R, P, D, L have the same meaning as in Appendix 1.1, and β and Ω are positive adjustment coefficients, j and ε are negative ones. The dynamics of the system is represented by the following three equations:

$$\text{(B.1)} \qquad \dot{P} = \beta[D_0 + \mathrm{d}D + R - PL] + \dot{P}^*$$

$$\text{(B.2)} \qquad \dot{P}^* = \Omega[R^* + D^* - P^*L^*]$$

$$\text{(B.3)} \qquad \dot{R} = j[R + D_0 + \mathrm{d}D - PL] + \varepsilon[P - P^*].$$

D_0 indicates the initial level of domestic assets owned by the central bank of the domestic country, d indicates a prime difference, $\mathrm{d}D$ is the once-and-for-all increase in D. For some particular values of the coefficients of adjustment we obtain Hume's price-specie flow; for some other values of the coefficients, we obtain the monetary-approach version of the adjustment.

Hume's view: $\beta > 0, j = 0, \varepsilon < 0, \Omega > 0$. In this case the adjustment happens through relative price level changes.

Monetary-approach view: $\beta = 0,\ j < 0,\ \Omega > 0$ and ε becomes irrelevant, since $\beta = 0$ implies that $P = P^*$. A value of β approaching zero is more realistic the smaller the home country.

In general, the smaller β and the higher j in absolute value, the more we come close to the monetary-approach view, and the larger β and the smaller j in absolute value the more we approach Hume's world.

Stability of the system

Call $D_0 + \mathrm{d}D = k_1$ and $D^* + \overline{R} = k_2$; k_1 and k_2 are constant throughout. By using the above simplification in the notation and remembering that $R + R^* = \overline{R}$, we get:[26]

(B.1′) $$(\delta+\beta L)P-\delta P^*-\beta R=\beta k_1$$

(B.2′) $$(\delta+\Omega L^*)P^*+\Omega R=\Omega k_2$$

(B.3′) $$(jL-\varepsilon)P+\varepsilon P^*+(\delta-j)R=jk_1.$$

Putting the above system in matrix form, we obtain:

$$\begin{bmatrix}\delta+\beta L & -\delta & -\beta\\ 0 & \delta+\Omega L^* & \Omega\\ jL-\varepsilon & \varepsilon & \delta-j\end{bmatrix}\begin{bmatrix}P\\ P^*\\ R\end{bmatrix}=\begin{bmatrix}\beta k_1\\ \Omega k_2\\ jk_1\end{bmatrix}$$

Solving the determinant of the matrix for δ and equating the resulting equation to zero we get:

$$\delta^3+\delta^2(\beta L+\Omega L^*-j)+\delta(\Omega L^*L\beta-\Omega L^*j-jL\Omega-\varepsilon\beta)$$
$$-\varepsilon\beta\Omega(L+L^*)=0$$

which can be simplified as follows:

$$a_0\delta^3+a_1\delta^2+a_2\delta+a_3=0.$$

The condition for stability of the system is:[27]

$$a_1>0 \quad \text{and} \quad a_1a_2-a_0a_3>0$$

which are both satisfied, as can be easily verified.

Simulations could be performed by attributing particular values to the parameters β, j, Ω and ε to see how the time path of the variables P, P^* and R changes when the parameters change.

An interesting subject to investigate is the probable effect of the size of the home country, of the ratio of traded to non-traded goods, of the degree of capital mobility and of other institutional factors (such as the speed at which arbitrage operates in equalising prices of the same commodities across countries) on the size of the various adjustment coefficients (β, j and ε).

This lies, however, outside the scope of this short appendix, whose only purpose was to show how the direct-expenditure effect and the price-specie flow are but two extreme versions of the same basic model and how they are compatible with each other.

NOTES TO CHAPTER 1

1. This is the most remarkable treatise in Italian economic literature on the balance of payments, and one of the most remarkable in economic literature in general. An English translation of the book can be found in *'Early Economic Thought'*, Monroe, Arthur E. (ed), Cambridge, Mass., Harvard University Press, 1924.
2. The direct-expenditure effect implies that a monetary expansion affects the balance of payments or the exchange rate directly without prior relative price-level changes bringing about the adjustment.
3. This is shown formally in Appendix 1.1.
4. See Genberg (1974) for a proof that, because of Walras' law, to concentrate on the money market in balance-of-payments analysis does not imply the exclusion of other markets.
5. See Section 5 below.
6. The debasement of a currency is equivalent to today's once-and-for-all increase in the nominal quantity of money. For the various methods of debasement and the advantages and disadvantages of each method, see Galiani (1750), 11, 112–14.
7. If traded goods only exist in every country, there is still the possibility that price levels differ across countries during the adjustment process if arbitrage does not operate instantaneously. It was probably such a world, with gold prices for the same goods differing across countries because of slow arbitrage, that Hume had in mind (Staley, 1976).
8. For authors prior to 1803, research was conducted from the series of 50 volumes edited by Pietro Custodi: *Scrittori Classici Italiani di Economia Politica*, Milan, 1803–16. In quotations from earlier authors, the page and the volume number refer to this series. The series is divided into two parts of 7 and 43 volumes each. For simplicity we have numbered the volumes progressively.
9. The exchange rate Serra refers to here is that of a silver coin of the Kingdom of Naples (Carlino), whose silver content had been reduced repeatedly during Serra's lifetime.
10. This framework has become fashionable in the early 1970s in theoretical and empirical investigations of the recent acceleration of world inflation (Genberg and Swoboda, 1977; Heller, 1976).
11. Abruzzo is a region of central Italy.
12. The wedge between income and expenditure, the relationship between stocks and flows, and the stock-adjustment nature of balance-of-payments disequilibria play a key role in the monetary approach to balance-of-payments theory. It is for this reason that the concept of 'hoarding' and a consumption function of the type introduced by Prais (1961), or the generalisation thereof used by Dornbusch (1975b) is so widely used in the monetary-approach literature.
13. 'Old idea' can be safely interpreted here as 'the expected price level'.
14. For Serra's quotation, see Section 2.
15. Assuming the domestic component of the base is not increased.
16. See also Appendix. 1.10.
17. The same result follows if a currency which is quoted in foreign exchange markets is debased, provided it is pegged by the government of the Kingdom.

18. For the outflow of gold and silver to occur, the monetary authorities must also peg the price of the domestic currency in terms of gold and silver.
19. Most of the ideas developed in this booklet are contained (in English) in his *The Economics of Inflation* (London, Allen & Unwin, 1937).
20. See in Section 5 quotations from Broggia, Pantaleoni, Pareto.
21. The same interpretation of Galiani's thought on this point is also found in F. Cesarano (1975).
22. See also paragraph 2 of this chapter.
23. Besides a transaction motive for holding money, Beccaria also had precautionary motive (money that lies 'dead and inactive', see paragraph 4). In addition, he seemed to have the interest rate level in his implicit demand function for money (see paragraph 2).
24. See, for instance, the work of Bresciani-Turroni.
25. The model is therefore partial-equilibrium; it is essentially the same as in Dornbusch (1975c).
26. The assumption of constancy of world reserves implies that the home country is not a reserve-currency country.
27. See Gandolfo (1971).

2 Fluctuations of the Italian Balance of Payments, 1951–73: An Econometric Analysis

INTRODUCTION

In this chapter empirical evidence which supports a monetary explanation of Italian balance-of-payments fluctuations from 1951 to 1973 is presented. The theoretical model underlying the tests is based on the monetary approach to the balance of payments as developed under the small-country assumption by Mundell (1971), Johnson (1958, 1973), and a number of their students.[1] Its main assumptions and implications, and its close similarities with the Italian tradition of balance-of-payments and exchange-rate theory, have already been outlined in detail in Chapter 1, and discussion of the derivation of the equations tested will therefore be very short.

In Section 1 the model is developed and empirical tests of the Italian balance of payments with annual and quarterly data are presented. The equation tested is derived assuming that the domestic price level cannot diverge from the world price level and that all goods are traded. However, the presence of non-traded goods might lead to a divergence of domestic and world price levels in the short and medium run, and even in the long run if productivity grows at different rates in the traded and non-traded sectors. A more complete model that included non-traded goods would be more realistic, but the gain in realism could only be achieved at the expense of simplicity, both in theoretical model building and econometric test procedures. We shall therefore adhere to the simpler model[2] and test the Itaian balance of payments on the main arguments of the demand and supply functions for money. The parameters of the balance-of-payments equation are estimated by the two-stage least-square method simultaneously with the parameters of a reaction function of the Bank of Italy, since one-stage least-square estimates of the coefficient of the domestic assets of the Bank of Italy in the balance-of-payments equation might be biased by attempts to pursue sterilisation policies.

In Section 2 the same theory is tested using a different procedure, i.e. by estimating demand functions for money in Italy and in the rest of the world, constructing measures of excess demand for money for Italy and for the rest of the world, and, finally, regressing the balance of payments on the current and lagged measures thus constructed.

The annual tests of both Sections 1 and 2 cover the period 1951–73, while the quarterly tests cover only the period 1960–I to 1973–III, owing to the lack of quarterly data prior to 1960. The quarterly tests have been performed separately for the first half of the 1960s and for the succeeding period up to 1973, because the period from about 1965 to 1973 has been characterised by much larger government budget deficits and larger changes in the effective exchange rate of the lira. The estimation of parameters of the model for the two separate periods gives rise to interesting comparisons which will be discussed in detail in Sections 1 and 2. The years following 1974 have not been included in the sample period, both because they have been disturbed by the oil crisis and because, with flexible exchange rates, the variable which the theory explains becomes the exchange rate.[3]

Section 3 summarises the main conclusions and indicates the direction for future work.

The tests presented in this chapter support the view that fluctuations of the Italian balance of payments in the post-war period, and particularly in the late 1960s and early 1970s, cannot be properly understood without explicit reference to the method of financing the government budget deficit and money market developments. Among Italian policy makers and economists this explanation of balance-of-payments fluctuations has few followers.[4] This is rather surprising when one considers the strength of the Italian tradition of classical balance-of-payments theory throughout the three and a half centuries up to about the first two or three decades of the twentieth century.

1. EMPIRICAL TESTS OF THE ITALIAN BALANCE OF PAYMENTS

As outlined in the previous chapter, the only two crucial assumptions of the monetary approach are the existence of arbitrage in at least some commodity markets and the stability of the demand function for money. Assuming, furthermore, that Italy is a 'small country', i.e. that it cannot influence the level of world prices and world interest rates, that all goods produced at home are traded, and that the time period considered is long enough to allow all markets to return to equilibrium after an initial disturbance,[5] one can specify the following system of equations:

$$(1) \qquad M^D = P[f(y, r)]$$

$$(2) \qquad M^S = a(DA + IR)$$

$$(3) \qquad M^S = M^D$$

where M^D is the quantity of money demanded, M^S the quantity supplied, P the price level, y real income, r the nominal interest, DA the domestic claims of the Bank of Italy, and IR the stock of international reserves.

Equation (1) is a standard demand function for money, homogeneous of degree one in prices, Equation (2) implies that base money is composed of domestic claims and of international reserves, and Equation (3) implies that the time period be long enough to allow all markets (including the money market) to reach equilibrium. The system of equations (1)–(3) does not exclude from the analysis the other markets relevant to the outcome of the balance of payments, since to the extent that one is interested only in the overall balance of payments and not in its subdivision between the current and the capital account, one can aggregate all other markets' excess supplies or demands by making use of Walras' law.

In the case in which a country makes frequent use of official loans (*prestiti compensativi*) to finance balance-of-payments deficits, equation (2) has to be rewritten as follows:

$$(2') \qquad M^s = a(DA + L) + aNIR$$

where L is the official foreign debt (stock) and $NIR = IR - L$ are net international reserves.

The variable y is assumed to be given exogeneously by population growth and the rate of technical change,[6] DA and a are assumed to be variables under the control of the monetary authorities, and P and r are assumed to be exogenously determined by the rest of the world (small-country assumption). L is assumed to be exogenously determined by the willingness of the rest of the world to lend and by the desire of the country in question to borrow. The system of equations (1), (2′), (3), determines, therefore, three variables: M^d, M^s and NIR. Substituting (1) and (2′) into (3), putting the resulting equations in terms of first differences and solving for $\mathrm{d}NIR = B$, where B is the balance of payments, one obtains:

$$(4) \qquad \frac{a}{M}B = \frac{1}{P}\,\mathrm{d}P + \frac{\eta y}{y}\,\mathrm{d}y - \frac{1}{a}\,\mathrm{d}a - \frac{a}{M}(\mathrm{d}DA + \mathrm{d}L) + \frac{\eta r}{r}\,\mathrm{d}r$$

where ηi is the elasticity of demand for money with respect to the variable $i(i = y, r)$, each with its natural sign ($\eta y > 0$, $\eta r < 0$).

Equation (4) states that the balance of payments is positively affected by the Italian price level (which under the small-country assumption is identical to the foreign price level) and by the growth of real income, and negatively by the monetary base multiplier and by the domestic assets of the Bank of Italy. As far as the sign of $\mathrm{d}P$ is concerned, an increase in the price level destroys real-money balances and increases the nominal quantity of money demanded. Therefore, given DA, the increased demand tends to be satisfied by reserve inflows. The increase in the productive capacity of the economy leads to an increase in the quantity of goods available for export and, hence, affects positively the balance of payments; this is equivalent to saying that the increase in real income increases the demand for money and that if the authorities do not satisfy the increased demand, the economy will import money from abroad via a balance-of-payments surplus. The surpluses of Germany, Japan and Italy during several years of the post-war period seem explicable in terms of rapid growth not fully matched by monetary policy.

An increase in a, on the other hand, affects the balance of payments negatively because it increases the supply of money, and, given the quantity demanded, the excess supply is eliminated via a deficit in the balance of payments. The signs of the coefficients $\mathrm{d}DA$ and $\mathrm{d}r$ can be explained in a similar fashion via their effect on the domestic money market.[7]

Equation (4) needs, however, to be modified in a number of ways before it can be tested.

(1) It is necessary to take account of the fact that the weighted average of the exchange rate of the lira with respect to the currencies of the rest of the world was not always constant during the period 1951–73, particularly in the latter part of the sample period. So that changes in exchange rates should not bias the estimated coefficients, a dummy variable was added to the explanatory variables of Equation (4), which is positive

when the lira descreased in value with respect to the currencies of the rest of the world, and negative in the opposite case. The dummy variable used was the weighted average of the rates of change of the exchange rates of the lira with respect to the currencies of twelve industrialised countries ($\dot{e}$). The expected sign of $\dot{e}$ is negative when the time intervals to which the data refer is short, positive when it is long. The reason for this is that devaluations (revaluations) have tended to occur in the quarters during which deficits (surpluses) were large, and this would tend to make the coefficient of $\dot{e}$ negative. The positive effect of the devaluation which the monetary theory predicts will be produced by the destruction of money balances, and financial assets need time to outweigh the statistical negative effect referred to above. Thus the longer the time period considered for the regressions, the more likely it is that the coefficient of $\dot{e}$ will be positive and significant.

(2) Equation (4) is derived under the long-run assumption that if exchange rates are fixed the Italian price level will be equal to the foreign price level. This assumption is clearly unrealistic for time intervals of a quarter, but it is also so for time intervals of a year because of the existence of non-traded goods and possibly of slow arbitrage in traded goods markets.[8] By focusing on the effect of increases in price level on the demand for money, long-run models of the monetary approach do not take into account the effect of changes in relative price levels on the balance of payments. In the real world when $\mathrm{d}P$ is large the competitiveness of Italian products worsens and, in addition, the real yield of financial and monetary assets in Italy is reduced. Both factors tend to worsen the balance of payments and reduce considerably the effect that higher prices have on the demand for money, and hence on the balance of payments.

(3) Once it is recognised that the real world departs from steady-state assumptions, the effect of the changes in real income on the balance of payments also becomes more complicated. On the one hand, there is the effect on which the monetary theory focuses its attention (namely, the effect of an increase in real income on the demand for money, and through this channel on the balance of payments); on the other, the impact effect of an increase in economic activity on the demand for imports must be recognised. This latter effect cannot be ignored in an economy such as the Italian, which is heavily dependent on imported capital goods for investment. It was therefore decided to isolate the impact effect of an increase in income from the longer-run monetary-approach effect, and to eliminate at the same time the independent price variable from the regressions by using as independent variables both the

increase in nominal income and the increase in permanent money income lagged one period.[9]

(4) Another variable added was the increase in the domestic component of the base of the rest of the world: dDA_w, obtained by adding the domestic source component of twelve industrial countries.[10] The inclusion of this variable is justified by the fact that the real world departs from steady-state assumptions. In the steady state, expansionary monetary policies by the rest of the world affect the small country's balance of payments via the world price level. Once adjustment lags are allowed for, there is room for a direct effect of dDA_w on B. It is reasonable to assume that the strength of the effect of dDA_w on B is proportional to the size of the country in question (see Appendix 2.2).

(5) Some experimentats with the changes in the ratio of high-powered money to money as a proxy for da did not give rise to significant coefficients. The reserve requirement ratio of commercial banks has been changed in Italy only on very rare occasions. However, until the reform of 1975, required reserves were composed not only of cash and deposits at the Bank of Italy but also of Treasury bills and both public and private bonds.[11] By changing the type of bonds subject to inclusion among required reserves, selective credit policies were pursued, but at the same time money market conditions were changed. Better proxies for da could have been devised, but given the great difficulties involved in the construction of an adjusted monetary-base series of commercial banks, it was decided to drop the variable from the regressions shown below.[12]

Taking into account modifications 1–5, Equation (4) becomes:[13]

$$(6) \quad B = \alpha_0 dY + \alpha_1 dY^P{}_{-1} + \alpha_2 dDA + \alpha_3 dr + \alpha_4 \dot{e} + \alpha_5 dDA_w$$

where $\alpha_0, \alpha_3 < 0_1, \alpha_1, \alpha_4, \alpha_5 > 0, \alpha_2 = -1$. Y is money income, Y^P permanent money income,[14] $\dot{e}$ is the weighted average of the rates of change of the exhange rates of the lira with respect to the currencies of twelve industrial countries, DA_w is the sum of the domestic assets of the central banks of the same twelve countries expressed in dollars, and the other variables have the same meaning as before.

The expected long-run coefficients are equal to:

$$\alpha_1 = \frac{M.\eta y}{aY^P}, \alpha_2 = -1, \alpha_3 = \frac{M\eta r}{ar}, \alpha_4 = \frac{M}{a}, \alpha_5 = \frac{M}{M_w}.e$$

There is no prediction for the size of the coefficient of $dY(\alpha_0)$.

The test of Equation (5) could yield a biased coefficient of α_2 if the Bank of Italy successfully sterilised reserves flow by changing its

Table 2.1 Two-stage least-square estimates of the parameters in equations (5) and (6). Italian balance of payments Annual data, 1951–73

Regressions 1 and 2

Interest rate used	dY	dY^{P}_{-1}	dDA	dr	$\dot{e}$	dDA_w	TFR	D	B
$d(r_G - r_{d/d})$	−0·15	0·40	−0·94	−172·29	8315·39	40·82	−0·44	557·73	−0·50
	(−3·51)	(9.49)	(−10·68)	(−2.15)	(4·23)	(5·87)	(−12·56)	(3·06)	(−4·43)
dr_F	−0·08	0·35	−1·04	−212·86	7740·32	40·66	−0·44	543·25	−0·51
	(−2·28)	(10·34)	(−15·71)	(−4·92)	(5·20)	(7·82)	(13·05)	(3·06)	(−4·70)

Regressions 3 and 4 (ordinary least-square estimates)

Interest rate used	dY	dY^{P}_{-1}	dDA	dr	$\dot{e}$	dDA_w	R^2	DW	SER	$\bar{x}$
$d(r_G - r_{d/d})$	−0·21	0·42	−0·75	−212·72	6535·89	29·89	0·93	2·12	229·47	517·4
	(−3·21)	(6·40)	(−6·16)	(−1·72)	(2·19)	(2·94)				
dr_F	−0·15	0·37	−0·84	−186·06	6136·30	30·12	0·94	1·99	218·98	517·4
	(−2·17)	(5·71)	(−7·26)	(−2·22)	(2·15)	(3·12)				

Note: The numbers in parenthesis are + − statistics, SER is the standard error of the regression and $\bar{x}$ is the average of the absolute value of the dependent variable.

domestic assets. In order to avoid the reverse causation problem between dDA and B, Equation (5) will be estimated simultaneously with a reaction function of the central bank. For the test on annual data the system of equations is therefore composed of Equations (5) and (6):

$$\mathrm{d}DA = \beta_0 TFR + \beta_1 D + \beta_2 B \qquad \beta_0, \beta_2 < 0 \qquad \beta_1 > 0$$

where TFR is the Treasury financing requirement, defined as revenues minus expenditure, and D is a dummy variable which assumes the values of -1 in the years 1958, 1959, 1970 and 1971 and zero for all other years of the sample period (1951–73). The years 1958, 1959, 1970 and 1971 were years in which a large fraction of the Treasury financing requirement was financed by sales of bonds to the public and/or to banks. In 1958, 1959 and 1971 interest rates were falling in the presence of a high demand for bonds, and in 1970 direct interventions in the bond market by the Bank of Italy were reduced, interest rates increased sharply, and the supply of bonds by the private sector fell to a very low level. This enabled the Bank of Italy to finance a smaller share of the government budget deficit than would otherwise have been the case. Table 2.1 contains the test of the system of equations (5) and (6) performed on annual data for the period 1951–53, as well as the tests of Equation (5) obtained by ordinary least squares. The two variables used for the opportunity cost of holding money are the difference between the medium-term government-bond yield and the interest rate paid on demand deposits ($r_G - r_{dd}$), and the interest rate on medium-term bonds issued by financial institutions (r_F). By using the simultaneous estimation procedure the t-statistics all come higher, but the coefficients are not very different (except for $\dot{e}$ and dDA_w), implying that, on the whole, reserve sterilisations have been unimportant. The tests confirm that the direction of causation runs mostly from the Treasury financing requirement to the domestic assets of the central bank to the balance of payments. The most striking finding is that the coefficients of dDA in Regressions 1 and 2 approximate the expected long-run value of -1, which implies a one-to-one substitution of domestic assets for foreign assets in the central bank's balance sheet within one year when expansionary monetary policies are pursued. All the other coefficients also have the expected sign.

As far as their size is concerned, the coefficient of dY^P_{-1} approximates its expected long-run value, while the coefficient of dDA_w is somewhat larger than expected, and the coefficient of $\dot{e}$ is about 40 percent lower than expected, since a devaluation probably takes more than one year to exert its full effect on the balance of payments.[15] The coefficient of the interest rate r_F is about 1/2 of the maximum expected value, while the coefficient of $d(r_G - r_{d/d})$ is considerably lower than expected. The rate r_F probably reflects the effect of higher inflation rates on the demand for money and financial assets better than a difference between two nominal rates. One would argue that the negative sign of the coefficient of dr_F might be due to the fact that the Bank of Italy has generally tended to increase the structure of interest rates in periods of balance-of-payments crisis as a defensive measure, i.e. that the direction of causality is from the balance of payments to r_F and not vice versa as implied by the monetary approach. If this were true, the coefficient of dr_F in the quarterly tests would have to be higher and more significant than in the annual tests, which is not the case, as the quarterly tests presented below show.

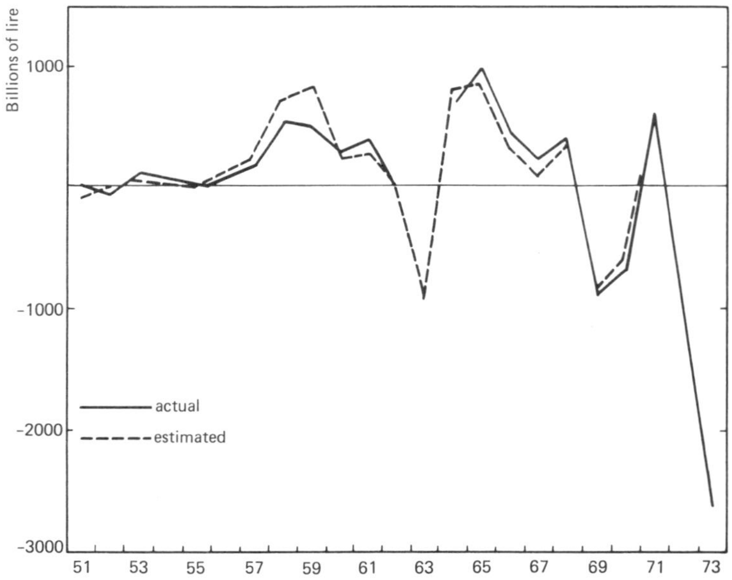

Fig. 2.1 Italian balance of payments (billions of lire). Regression 2, Table 2.1

Figure 2.1 shows the actual and expected value obtained from regression 2 of Table 2.1. By inspection of Figure 2.1 it can be seen that the Italian payments crises of 1963, 1969–70, and 1972–3 are explained very well by the model.

We now move on to the presentation of the tests performed on quarterly data for the separate periods 1960–I to 1967–II and 1966–IV to

1973–III.[16] The system of equations estimated simultaneously by the two-stage least-square method is:

$$(7)\qquad B = \alpha_0 \mathrm{d}Y + \alpha_1 \mathrm{d}Y^P{}_{-1} + \alpha_2 \mathrm{d}DA + \alpha_3 \mathrm{d}DA_{-1} + \alpha_4 \dot{e} + \\ + \alpha_5 \dot{e}_{-1} + \alpha_6 \mathrm{d}DA_w + \alpha_7 \mathrm{d}DA_{w-1} + \alpha_8 \mathrm{d}r \\ \alpha_0, \alpha_2, \alpha_3, \alpha_4, \alpha_8 < 0, \alpha_1, \alpha_5, \ \alpha_6, \alpha_7 > 0$$

$$(8)\qquad \mathrm{d}DA = \beta_0 TFR + \beta_1 \mathrm{d}r_F + \beta_2 D_1 + \beta_3 D_3 + \beta_4 D_4 + \beta_5 B + \beta_6 B_{-1} \\ \beta_0, \beta_5, \beta_6 < 0;\ \beta_1 > 0$$

where D_1, D_3, D_4 are seasonal dummy variables relating to the first, third, and fourth quarter, respectively, and r_F is the interest rate on medium-term bonds issued by financial institutions. Since during the first period the variable $\dot{e}$ was almost always equal to zero, it was neglected. In that period, the only measure for the opportunity cost of holding money which gave relatively satisfactory results was the rate of inflation (not the first difference). The quarter-to-quarter changes in interest rates were probably too small to exert a significant influence on the balance of payments.

Table 2.2 contains the two-stage least-square estimates of parameters in Equations (7) and (8).

For the first period the inclusion of the change in permanent income was not necessary, as $\mathrm{d}Y$ already reflects the positive effect of increased income on the balance of payments (via the demand for money). This is probably explained by the fact that nominal income grew at a relatively more stable rate in that period. The coefficient of $\mathrm{d}Y$ is about 40 percent lower than its long-run value.[17] The sum of the coefficients of $\mathrm{d}DA$ show that the effect of expansionary monetary policies on the balance of payments contrasts sharply with the evidence obtained from the second period in which exchange rates were not perfectly fixed (see below).

The sum of the coefficients of $\mathrm{d}DA_w$ is about three times as large as its expected long-run value. This is in agreement with what was found when testing the monetary theory for the US balance of payments.[18] In the case of the United States an increase in domestic assets in one year generates a deficit in the balance of payments in the same year which is larger than the expected long-run deficit.

As a US balance-of-payments deficit corresponds to a surplus in the rest of the world, a larger than expected coefficient of the changes in domestic assets of the Federal Reserve System in the US balance-of-payments equation also implies a larger than expected coefficient of $\mathrm{d}DA_w$ in the Italian balance of payments. This finding has important

Table 2.2 Two-stage least-square estimates of the parameters in equations (7) and (8). Italian balance of payments. Quarterly data

Regression 5 (quarterly data, 1960–I to 1967–II)

α_0 dY	α_2 dDA	α_3 dDA_{-1}	α_6 dDA_w	α_7 dDA_{w-1}	α_8 $\dot{p}$	β_0 TFR	β_1 dr_F	β_2 D_1	β_3 D_3	β_4 D_4	D_{63}	β_5 B	β_6 B_{-1}
(0·29)	−0·88	−0·45	75·27	21·68	−4782·0	−0·27	205·0	−204·0	−129·0	299·0	208·0	−0·5	0·0
(1·19)	(−5·19)	(−2·26)	(3·85)	(1·29)	(−1·07)	(−1·39)	(0·84)	(−2·45)	(−1·32)	(2·54)	(1·97)	(−0·18)	(0·0)

Regression 6 (quarterly data, 1966–IV to 1973–III)

α_0 dY	α_1 dY^y_{-1}	α_2 dDA	α_3 dDA_{-1}	α_4 $\dot{e}$	α_5 $\dot{e}_{-1}$	α_8 dr_F	β_0 TRF	β_1 dr_F	β_2 D_1	β_3 D_3	β_4 D_4	β_5 B	β_6 B_{-1}
−0·35	0·86	−0·33	−0·31	−9150·0	3058·0	−164·39	−0·77	593·67	−739·36	−859·97	498·45	0·63	−0·3
(−1·79)	(2·90)	(−2·74)	(−2·73)	(−4·77)	(1·27)	(−1·26)	(−5·01)	(2·43)	(−4·80)	(−3·92)	(2·45)	(1·84)	(−1·0)

Note: The numbers in parenthesis are + − statistics.

implications for the sources and transmission of world inflation. It implies that under perfectly fixed exchange rates, and with the dollar as a reserve currency, an important source of increase in world reserves has been the acquisition of domestic assets by the Federal Reserve System and that the monetary policy of the Federal Reserve System has affected the money stock of the rest of the world, with a short lag. Genberg[19] has found that European inflation has led US inflation by about two to three years, which seems to fit the above explanation.

The coefficients of B and B_{-1} are not significantly different from zero, which implies that changes in the domestic assets of the central bank have not reacted to balance-of-payments surpluses or deficits, and that the direction of causation runs from the domestic assets to the balance of payments. In addition to the seasonal dummy variables, we have included in the reaction function a dummy variable D_{63} which reflects the large increase in domestic assets resulting from the policy adopted by the central bank in the face of the unusual wage push of 1963 (the 1963 Italian balance-of-payments crisis). D_{63} is equal to 1 in the four quarters of 1963 and in the first quarter of 1964, and zero otherwise.

The Treasury financing requirement did not exert a strong influence on changes in domestic assets, in sharp contrast with the following period in which it became the dominant variable in the explanation of the balance of payments (cf. the coefficients and significance of TFR in Regressions 5 and 6 in Table 2.2).

The greater instability of all the variables in the period 1966–IV to 1973–III compared with the previous period has given rise to data that clearly bring out some important aspects of the monetary theory of the balance of payments (see Regression 6, Table 2.2).

As already pointed out, the Treasury financing requirement became the variable which most clearly influenced balance-of-payments fluctuations. Furthermore, the duality between the monetary theory of the balance of payments and the monetary theory of exchange-rate changes implies that at a time of large and frequent movements of exchange rates, it is the the exchange rate that becomes the dependent variable of the system rather than the balance of payments. It follows that under an international monetary system in which exchange rates are allowed to be more flexible, the effect of $\mathrm{d}DA$ and $\mathrm{d}DA_w$ on the balance of payments is necessarily reduced. Indeed, in Regression 6 the coefficients of $\mathrm{d}DA_w$ and $\mathrm{d}DA_{w-1}$ are no longer significant and the coefficients of $\mathrm{d}DA$ and $\mathrm{d}DA_{-1}$ are almost halved with respect to the previous period. The sum of the coefficients of $\mathrm{d}DA$ implies that about 60 percent of the domestic assets created by the Bank of Italy 'leaked' through the balance of payments in six months. Besides the greater flexibility of exchange rates, the frequent *ad hoc* measures taken during this period, when the balance of payments was worsening, might also help to explain the lower coefficients of dDA and dDA_{-1}. Measures such as limits to the purchase of foreign exchange by tourists, controls on banks' and individuals' capital movements and so forth, tend to disrupt the relationship between dDA and B.

The two-stage least-square estimates of the reaction function indicate that the pegging of nominal interest rates pursued by the monetary authorities in the second period resulted in a much larger fraction of the Treasury financing requirement having to be financed by the creation of high-powered money. Furthermore, there is no evidence of quarter-to-quarter sterilisation of reserve flows, since the coefficient of $B(\beta_5)$ is positive.

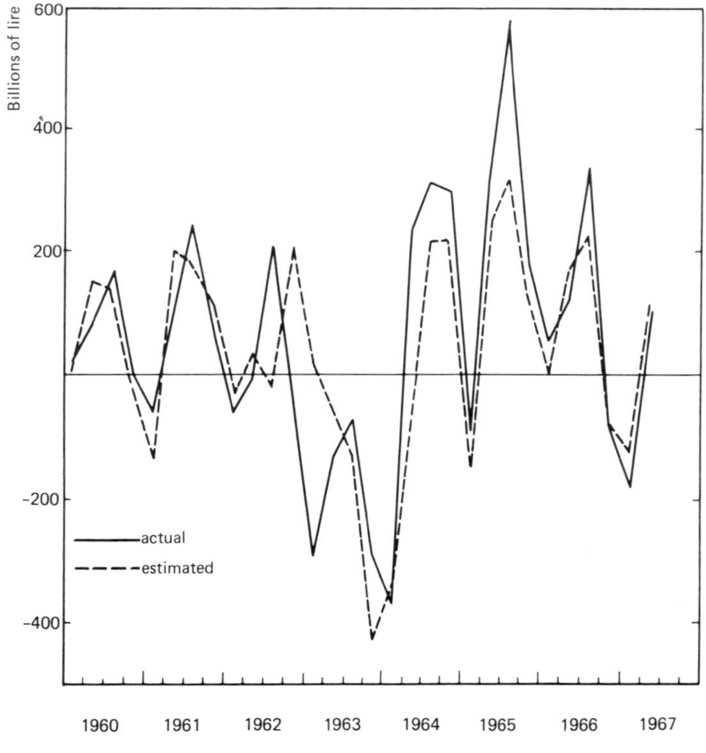

Fig. 2.2 Italian quarterly balance of payments (billions of lire). Regression 5, Table 2.2

Figure 2.2 shows the estimated quarterly balance of payments obtained from Regression 5, and Figure 2.3 the estimated balance of payments obtained from Regression 6 (Table 2.2). In both figures the actual values are usually considerably greater than those expected in the third quarter of the year because of reserve inflows from tourism (especially in the second half of the 1960s). A dummy variable which assumes values of 1 in the third quarter and zero otherwise was introduced in the estimates of the quarterly balance of payments (not

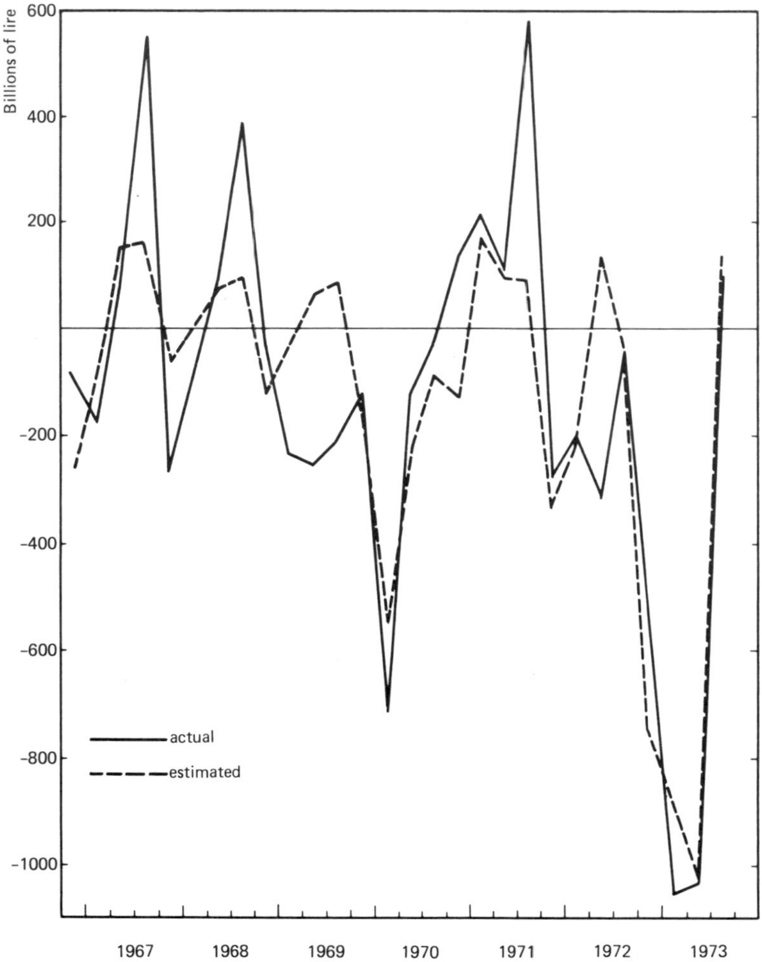

Fig. 2.3 Italian quarterly balance of payments (billions of lire). Regression 6, Table 2.2

shown here) and the explanatory power of the regressions thereby considerably improved.

The theory outlined in this chapter seems to offer a convincing explanation of the three Italian payments crises of 1963, 1969–70, and 1972–3, as may be seen from Figure 2.1. The quarterly tests also show that the estimated balance of payments followed the downswings and upswings of the actual balance of payments quite closely (see Figures 2.2 and 2.3), with only a few exceptions. In the first two quarters of 1963 the fit is relatively poor and the estimated value seems to follow with a lag of one quarter the actual values, which might indicate the presence of capital outflows connected with an expected devaluation of the lira (see Figure 2.2). Italian banknote remittances, a very sensitive indicator of capital outflows, did in fact peak in the first half of the year.[20]

The quarterly fit is also relatively poor in 1969 (see Figure 2.3), probably because the troubles connected with the expiry of important labour contracts in the last quarter of the year, in a tense labour market, were anticipated, and capital started to flow out of the country. In 1969 net capital outflows were indeed more than twice those of 1968. Fiscal considerations and an expected revaluation of the German mark may also have been relevant factors affecting net capital outflows.[21]

2. ALTERNATIVE TESTS OF THE ITALIAN BALANCE OF PAYMENTS

In this section the relevance of disturbances in the money market to balance-of-payments analysis is investigated by regressing the Italian balance of payments on current and lagged measures of *ex ante* flow excess demand for money. To construct these measures the demand functions for M_1 and M_2 have been tested for Italy and a group of twelve industrialised countries.[22] The measures constructed for the foreign countries are then aggregated to obtain a measure relating to the rest of the world.

Assuming that the actual real stock of money adjusts with a lag to the discrepancy between desired and actual real holdings of money, one can write:

$$(9) \qquad \ln m_t - \ln m_{t-1} = \lambda[\ln m_t^* - \ln m_{t-1}] \qquad \lambda > 0$$

where λ indicates the adjustment parameter of actual to desired real balances, ln stands for the natural logarith, m_t the actual money stock at time t in real terms, and m_t^* the real desired money stock at time t.

It is assumed that the desired money stock depends on real income and the opportunity cost of holding money. In order to keep the calculations as simple as possible, variables such as population growth or inflation are neglected:

$$\ln m_t^* = \alpha + \beta \ln y_t + \gamma \ln(r_G - r_{d/d})_t \tag{10}$$

where r_G represents the interest rate on government bonds and $r_{d/d}$ the interest rate paid on demand deposits; y_t is real income. By substitution of (10) into (9) one obtains:

$$\ln m_t = a + b \ln y_t + c \ln (r_G - r_{d/d})_t + d \ln m_{t-1} \tag{11}$$

Table 2.3 contains the tests of Equation (11) for money narrowly defined (m_1), money broadly defined (m_2), and demand deposits, all deflated by the consumer price index. $b/(1-d) = b/\lambda$ is an estimate of the long-run income elasticity of $m_i (\beta)$ and $c/(1-d) = c/\lambda$ is an estimate of the long-run interest elasticity of $m_i(\gamma)$.

Table 2.3 Ordinary least-square estimates of equation (11). Annual data, 1950–73

Dependent variable (ln)	ln y	ln $(r_G - r_{d/d})$	ln m_{i-1}	R^2	D.W.
m_1	0·07	−0·10	0·94	0·999	1·65
	(1·40)	(−2·21)	(18·71)		
m_2	0·08	−0·06	0·93	0·999	1·72
	(1·74)	(−1·41)	(20·01)		
Demand deposits					
m_3	0·07	−0·11	0·94	0·999	1·55
	(1·73)	(−1·92)	(21·07)		

Note: The numbers in parenthese are t-statistics.

The measures of excess demand for money used as independent variables in the balance-of-payments regression are defined as follows: *ex ante* flow excess demand for m_i:[23]

$$\text{(12)} \qquad \left[\dot{m}^*_{i.t} - \left(\frac{\dot{DA}}{P}\right)_t\right] M_{i.t-1} = EDM_i$$

where a dot indicates a percentage change and $m^*_{i.t}$ is the desired long-run real-money stock calculated by using the elasticities of Table 2.4. DA are the domestic assets of the Bank of Italy, whose changes reflect *ex post* the overall thrust of Italian monetary policy, since the Italian monetary authorities cannot control the nominal money stock under fixed exchange rates except in the very short run. M_i is equal to $P_i m_i$ where P_i is the consumer price index.[24]

Table 2.4 Long-run elasticities of demand for money and demand deposits (from Table 2.3)

	Constant	Income elasticity	Interest elasticity
m_1	–	1·24	–1·73
m_2	–	1·17	–0·84
Demand deposits	–	1·17	–1·83

The balance-of-payments equation to be tested is:

$$\text{(13)} \qquad B = h + f\,EDM_i + g\,\dot{e} + u$$

where B is the balance of payments corrected both for foreign loans obtained by Italian firms and by the Bank of Italy for balance-of-payments purposes (which in the Italian balance-of-payments accounts are registered above the line as autonomous transactions and, $\dot{e}$ indicates a dummy variable which is positive when the lira has decreased in value in terms of the currencies of Italy's main trading partners and negative when it has increased in value. The introduction of $\dot{e}$ is necessary, as devaluations (revaluations) have tended to occur in the post-war period when balance-of-payments deficits (surpluses) have grown very large. Its exclusion could bias the coefficient of f.[25] The constant term is represented by h. The expected signs of the coefficients are $f > 0$ and $g < 0$. Although the monetary theory of the balance of payments predicts a positive effect of $\dot{e}$ on B, g might still be negative if the predicted positive effect cannot outweigh the deficit accumulated from the beginning of the year (or quarter) until the day of the devaluation.

The basic idea of the monetary approach is that a surplus in the balance of payments is connected either with a stock adjustment in the money market or with a continuous flow disturbance such as real growth and an insufficient increase of the domestic asset holdings of the central bank. If one assumes that the demand for money is stable, and that no political disturbances occur, stock adjustments can be ruled out as empirically irrelevant.

Equation (13) therefore incorporates the fundamental proposition that in a stable environment balance-of-payments surpluses or deficits can occur only as a consequence of continuous flow disturbances. The monetary approach does not rule out *a priori* that the direction of causation could be from the balance of payments to the domestic money market, and that this might be the relevant chain of causation for some countries[26] and for some time periods.[27] The tests presented in the previous section seem to indicate, however, that in the case of Italy's balance of payments in the period under analysis, the direction of causation was largely from domestic monetary disturbances to the balance of payments, and not the other way around.

Table 2.5 Italian balance of payments on ex ante *flow-excess demand for money Annual data, 1951–73*

No. of regr.	Definition of money	Constant	EDM_i	$\dot{e}$	R^2	DW
7	Demand deposits	110·54 (1·25)	0·00142 (4·54)	– 16361·0 (– 5·50)	0·74	2·22
8	Demand deposits		0·00137 (4·36)	– 15708·0 (– 5·29)	0·72	2·04
9	M_1		0·00096 (4·17)	– 15649·0 (– 5·16)	0·71	2·07
10	M_2	159·70 (1·68)	0·00760 (4·16)	– 13870·0 (– 4·29)	0·72	1·99

Note: Numbers in parenthesis are + – statistics

Table 2.5 contains the tests of Equation (11) on annual data from 1951 to 1973. Where the constant terms does not appear it was not significant. *Ex post* flow excess demand for money measures[28] also gave satisfactory results (see Table 2.6), but their explanatory power is slightly less than that of *ex ante* flow measures.

The coefficients of the excess demands are usually significant as expected, although the demand functions used exclude possibly important variables like population growth or the rate of inflation. The regressions of Table 2.5 and Table 2.6 indicate that the excess demand for M_2 seems to possess a marginally higher explanatory power than the excess demand for M_1.[29]

Table 2.6 Italian balance of payments on ex post *flow-excess demand for money. Annual data, 1951–73*

No. of regr.	Definition of money	Constant	EDM_i	ED for M_2 in rest of world*	$\dot{e}$	R^2	DW
11	M_2		0·0009	−0·32	−19126·0	0·57	2·11
			(2·17)	(−2·17)	(−5·11)		
12	M_2	110·55	0·0010	−0·35	−19994·0	0·58	2·25
		(0·97)	(2·31)	(−2·31)	(−5·19)		
13	Currency and demand deposits		0·013/0·005	−0·712	−21015·0	0·63	1·89
			(1.67)/(1.10)	(−2.34)	(−5.51)		
14		114·76	0·014/0·005		−2085	0.66	2.04
		(1·09)	(1·94)/(1·07)		(−5·45)		
15			0·014/0·005		−19992·0	0·64	1·90
			(1·82)/(1·03)		(−5·35)		

Note: Numbers in parenthesis are *t*-statistics.
* The estimates of the demand functions for M_2 for the twelve foreign countries are not reported here because of space limitations. The interested reader can consult Tullio (1979c).

Table 2.7 contains regressions of the quarterly Italian balance of payments on current and lagged excess demand for M_1 and M_2. The Almon polynomial lag estimation technique was used (the polynomials are all of the second order and no constraints are imposed on them). Excess demand in the money market exerts its effect on the balance of payments within three quarters. The results are not substantially different for M_1 and M_2, although the market for M_2 seems to be somewhat more closely correlated to the balance of payments, as was also the case with the annual data. *Ex ante* measures are again superior to *ex post* measures; the constant term was never significantly different from zero and therefore does not appear in the regressions.[30]

By regressing the quarterly Italian balance of payments on quarterly measures of excess demand for M_1 and M_2 separately for the periods 1960–III to 1967–II and 1966–IV to 1973–III one finds that in the first period excess demands for money tended to influence the balance of payments to a much larger extent. As has been argued in the previous section, the latter result is probably a consequence of (a) greater

Table 2.7 Italian balance of payments on excess demand for money. Quarterly data, 1961–I to 1973–III

No. of regr.		M_1 *ex-ante*		$\dot{e}$	R^2	D.W.	S.E.R.
	t	0·00008	(1·34)	−71·21.(−3·76)	0·50	1·58	248·30
	$t-1$	0·00022	(4·33)	−35·65.(−1·81)			
16	$t-2$	0·00019	(3·65)				
	$t-3$	−0·00001	(−0·11)				
	Sum:	0·00048					
		M_2 *ex-ante*					
	t	0·00015	(1·49)	−60·30.(−3·39)	0·55	1·65	233·55
	$t-1$	0·00043	(5·17)	−33·85.(−1·75)			
17	$t-2$	0·00036	(4·33)				
	$t-3$	−0·00003	(−0·25)				
	Sum:	0·00091					
		M_2 *ex-post*					
	t	0·00014	(1·66)	−59·76.(−2·96)	0·48	1·44	251·29
	$t-1$	0·00048	(4·04)	−43·87.(−2·13)			
18	$t-2$	0·00045	(3·62)				
	$t-3$	0·00005	(0·32)				
	Sum:	0·00112					

Note: Numbers in parenthesis are t-statistics.
Average of absolute values of dependent variable = 245·00

fluctuations of exchange rates in the second period, and (b) more *ad hoc* measures in that period to reduce private demand for foreign exchange.[31] The quarterly tests for the two sub-periods are not shown here because of limitations of space.

The indirect tests of this section confirm that any serious analysis of the Italian balance of payments cannot abstract from money-market conditions. Although the direction of causation might be from the balance of payments to the money market, this is not the case for Italy, as the tests presented in Section 1 show.

3. CONCLUSIONS

In this chapter empirical evidence in favour of adopting the monetary approach to the balance of payments to explain Italian balance-of-payments fluctuations in the post-war period has been presented.

The main shortcoming of the model tested is that the role and behaviour of the prices of non-traded goods is neglected. Another unsatisfactory aspect is that annual or quarterly income growth is assumed to be independent of the monetary policy pursued. It can be justified on a theoretical level on the grounds that our knowledge of the transmission mechanism of monetary policy is still limited, and on an empirical level on the grounds that monetary policy seems to affect the balance of payments to a greater degree and more quickly than it does income. One could also justify the assumption on empirical grounds by noting that in the period under consideration the percentage changes in the domestic assets of the Bank of Italy have, on average, been much larger than the percentage changes of GNP.

The elimination of both these shortcomings involves the use of complicated dynamic disequilibrium models whose economic tests involve a loss of simplicity compared with the tests presented here.[32]

One criticism which is often made of direct tests of the monetary approach, such as those presented in Section 1, is that one is actually testing an identity and not a true behaviour relationship. The criticism seems unjustified for a number of reasons: (a) there is a demand-for-money function as well as a supply-of-money function involved in the estimation of balance-of-payments equations, and it seems far-fetched to consider the balance-of-payments equation (5) as an identity; (b) the further away the real world is from the long-run steady state, the less the equation tested can be considered an identity, because underlying markets are constantly in the process of reaching a new equilibrium and time lags disrupt the alleged identity; (c) by testing the equation by the two-stage least-square method, the changes in domestic assets used in the regressions are not the actual ones taken from the balance sheet of the central bank. In addition, the introduction of variables relating to the rest of the world (dDA_w) break the alleged identity even further. Nevertheless, in Section 2 the monetary theory of the balance of payments has been tested using a different method in order to overcome this criticism. It is interesting to note that although the tests of Section 2 offer interesting insights as to which is the relevant monetary aggregate and what are the relevant time lags between money-market developments and the balance of payments, the tests of Section 1 are more interesting, and perhaps more important for policy prescriptions, because they give some tentative indication as to the strength of the effect of each relevant independent variable on the balance of payments.

The analysis presented has not tried to identify the determinants of the fluctuations in the Treasury financing requirement which, particularly from the late 1960s onwards, has been the variable dominating balance-of-payments fluctuations, nor has it taken into account the role of trade unions in bringing about fluctuations of dDA. There is little doubt that social tensions can render DA partly endogenous (or even totally so, if the objective of pegging nominal interest rates is pursued). However, a government can to some extent always control dDA compatibly with pursuing the objective of full employment if only it has the will or the political power to do so. Whatever the determinants of movements of the domestic assets of the Bank of Italy, this study supports the 'hard version' of the monetary approach for the explanation of Italian payments fluctuations up to 1973, i.e. deficits have arisen from excessive domestic monetary expansion compared to both the real growth of the economy and foreign monetary expansion. This implies that the Italian foreign trade sector and Italian capital movements have been inherently stable during the period under study. On the other hand, since the sharp increase in the price of oil exerted a significant impact on the 1974 Italian balance of payments, for that year the direction of causation runs, at least partly, from the balance of payments to the domestic money market. The year 1974 was for this reason left out of the sample period.

Given the great importance for balance-of-payments analysis of the determinants of fluctuations of the domestic assets of the Bank of Italy, the following chapter will be devoted to a detailed analysis of the behaviour of monetary authorities in relation to the financing of budget deficits and to interest rates, especially from 1960 onwards. The following chapter may therefore be seen as complementary to the present one.

APPENDIX 2.1 SYMBOLS AND SOURCES OF DATA USED

m = M/P = money stock in real terms; M_1 is line 34 of IFS and M_2 line 34 plus line 35; P is the consumer price index (line 64).

y = Y/P = real GNP. The annual Y is line 99a of the *International Financial Statistics* of the International Monetary Fund, the quarterly one is an unpublished series taken from *Istituto Studi per la Congiuntura*.

r_G = medium-term government bond yield (line 61b of *IFS*).

$r_{d/d}$ = average interest rates paid on demand deposits. Bank of Italy; unpublished series.

i = long-term government bond yield (line 61a of *IFS*).

r_F = interest rate on medium-term bonds issued by financial institutions (*istituti di credito mobiliare*); *Bollettino Banca d'Italia.*

DA = domestic assets of the Bank of Italy, line 12a and line 12e of IFS.

e = rate of change of the Italian lira with respect to the currencies of twelve industrialised countries weighted with the Italian imports from each country. The twelve countries are: the United States, the United Kingdom, France, Germany, Switzerland, Japan, Sweden, Australia, Canada, Belgium, Holland and Denmark.

B = $dNIR_I$ = Italian balance of payments net of loans obtained from foreigners for balance-of-payments purposes (*prestiti compensativi*), which in the Italian balance-of-payments accounts are registered above the line as autonomous transactions. The official balance of payments is found in the *Bollettino Banca d'Italia.*

y_t^P = permanent real GNP = $\sum_{i=0}^{4} w_i y_{t-i}$, where the set of geometrically declining weights chosen arbitrarily is: $w_0 = 0{\cdot}60$, $w_1 = 0{\cdot}25$, $w_2 = 0{\cdot}10$, $w_3 = 0{\cdot}04$, $w_4 = 0{\cdot}01$. No attempt was made to find the R^2 maximising set of weights and the same set was used for quarterly, annual, nominal and real data.

Y_t^P = permanent nominal GNP = $\sum_{i=0}^{4} w_i Y_{t-i}$, where the weights w_i are the same as those used to compute y_t^P.

dL = loans obtained for balance-of-payments purposes and not sterilised by the Bank of Italy.

DA_w = $\sum_{j=1}^{12} DA_j$ = domestic assets of the rest of the world in dollar terms. DA_j = domestic assets of the central bank of country j converted into dollars at the 1950 exchange rate. All data were taken from IFS and the twelve countries are the same as those above (see $\dot{e}$).

TFR = Treasury financing requirement, defined as revenues minus expenditures. Bank of Italy; unpublished series.

a = M_2/H = money multiplier, where H is line 14 of IFS (reserve money).

APPENDIX 2.2 TENTATIVE CALCULATION OF THE EXPECTED SIZE OF THE COEFFICIENTS OF THE INDEPENDENT VARIABLES IN THE BALANCE-OF-PAYMENTS EQUATIONS OF SECTION 2.1

ANNUAL REGRESSIONS

Average value	1951–1973
M_2	$\approx$ 25133 billion lire
a	$\approx$ 1·85
Y^P_{-1}	$\approx$ 29200 billion lire
DA	$\approx$ 4000 billion lire
r_F	$\approx$ 6·62 percent
$(r_G - r_{d/d})$	$\approx$ 3·92 per cent

In addition assume that the income elasticity of demand for money (η_y) is equal to 1·2, the elasticity of the demand for money with respect to r_F is equal to $-0{\cdot}20$ and with respect to $(r_G - r_{d/d})$ is equal to -1 (see also Table 2.4).

The expected coefficients are:

$$\alpha_1 = (\text{coefficient of } dY^P_{-1}) = \frac{M_2\eta_y}{aY^P_{t-1}} \approx 0{\cdot}56$$

$$\alpha_2 = (\quad ,, \quad ,, \quad \mathrm{d}DA) \approx -1$$

$$\alpha_4 = (\quad ,, \quad ,, \quad \dot{e}) = \frac{M_2}{a} \approx 13585{\cdot}0$$

$$\alpha_5 = (\quad ,, \quad ,, \quad \mathrm{d}DA_w) = \mathrm{e}\cdot\frac{M_2}{M_w} = \frac{M_2}{M_w}\cdot 625 \approx 32$$

$$\alpha_3 = (\quad ,, \quad ,, \quad \mathrm{d}r_F) = -\frac{M_2}{a}\frac{0{\cdot}2}{r_F} = -410{\cdot}0$$

QUARTERLY REGRESSIONS

Average value	1960-I to 1967-II	1966-IV to 1973-III
M_2	20300	52500
a	1·89	2·46
Y^P_{-1}	28800	55700
DA	2700	9000
r_F	—	7·48

	1960-I to 1967-II	1966-IV to 1973-III
Coefficient of $Y^P_{-1} = \frac{M_2}{a} \cdot \frac{\eta_y}{Y^P_{t-1}}$	0·45	0·46
Sum of coefficients of dDA	−1	−1
" " " " $dDA_w = \frac{M_2}{M_w} e$	30	34
Coefficient of $dr_F = \frac{M_2}{a} \frac{0{\cdot}2}{r_F}$	—	570
Sum of coefficients of $\dot{e} = \frac{M_2}{a}$	—	21341

NOTES TO CHAPTER 2

1. See Frenkel, J. A., and Johnson, Harry G. (1976).
2. For empirical tests in which non-traded goods are taken into account, see Blejer (1975).
3. In Chapter 4, however, the monetary approach will be extended to the flexible exhange-rate case, and the fluctuations of the lira and Swiss franc exchange rate from 1973 to 1978 will be explained.
4. Two exceptions are Baffi (1968, 1975), Governor of the Bank of Italy from 1975, and in the early post-war period Bresciani-Turroni (1954).
5. Both the assumption that all goods are traded and the assumption that the time period considered is long enough to allow all markets to return to equilibrium will be relaxed later on.
6. The assumption that y is exogenously determined (and hence independent of monetary policy) reflects the classical belief in a vertical long-run Phillips curve. It constitutes a major shortcoming of the model. However, it can be justified theoretically on the grounds that our knowledge of the transmission mechanism of monetary policy is still limited, and empirically on the grounds that the effect of monetary policy on the balance of payments seems to be stronger and faster than the effect on real income. One could also justify the assumption on empirical grounds by noting that in the period under analysis the variability of DA has been on average larger than that of y.
7. It should be noted, however, that the coefficient of dr is equal to $\eta r/r$ only when domestic interest rates change, with foreign rates remaining unchanged. Otherwise, it is equal to zero if the domestic country and the rest of world have the same demand functions for money. In general, the coefficient will therefore be expected to be between zero and $\eta r/r$.
8. See Chapter 1 for a detailed analysis of the price-specie flow versus the direct-expenditure effect.
9. It should be pointed out, however, that when the rate of growth of current money income (Y) is used as an independent variable in annual regressions, its coefficient is always positive:

$$\frac{a}{M} \cdot B = \underset{(-4\cdot22)}{0\cdot50} \, (\mathrm{d}DA + \mathrm{d}L)\frac{a}{M} - \underset{(-2\cdot07)}{0\cdot12} \quad (r_G \dot{-} r_{d/d}) \rightarrow$$

$$+ \underset{(2\cdot24)}{0\cdot19} \, \dot{Y}$$

$R^2 = 0\cdot57$ $\quad DW = 1\cdot27$ $\quad ER = 0\cdot033$

where a dot above the variable indicates a precentage change, Y is GNP at current prices, and $r_G - r_{d/d}$ is the opportunity cost of holding money. For the meaning of symbols and the sources of the data used, see Appendix 2.1.

10. The twelve countries are the United States, the United Kingdom, France, Germany, Switzerland, Japan, Sweden, Australia, Canada, Belgium, Holland, and Denmark.
11. See also Chapter 3, Section 2 for a more detailed analysis of the money supply process in Italy.
12. A series of the adjusted monetary base calculated by the Bank of Italy is now available, but only for a part of the sample period on which the tests presented here are based.
13. It should be noted that only non-sterilised foreign official loans should be added to d*DA* and that the Bank of Italy sterilised a large fraction of total compensating loans. If non-sterilised loans are added to d*DA* the coefficient is only slightly reduced and its significance is largely unaffected. Therefore, in most of the regressions which follow d*L* has not been added to d*DA*.
14. See Appendix 2.1 for the method used to calculate permanent money income.
15. See Appendix 2.2 for a tentative calculation of the expected size of the coefficients.
16. The year 1966 marks the beginning of official interventions in the bond market by the Bank of Italy to peg interest rates. The two sub-periods overlap so as to acquire a greater degree of freedom.
17. See Appendix 2.2 for a tentative calculation of the expected size of the coefficients.
18. See Tullio (1979a).
19. See Genberg (1975), Chapter 2, Figure 1, p. 47.
20. See Table 72 of *Relazione Annuale, Banca d'Italia*, 1963, p. 192.
21. See *Relazione Annuale, Banca d'Italia*, 1969, p. 190.
22. The twelve countries are the same as in the previous section. See Note 9.
23. Blejer (1975) uses basically the same measures.
24. Symbols and sources of data used are summarised in Appendix 2.1.
25. $\dot{e}$ is the weighted average of the rates of change of the exchange rates of the lira with respect to twelve of Italy's main trading partners. See also Appendix 2.1.
26. In the case of Egypt, for instance, Bresciani-Turroni (1934) argues correctly that the direction of causation is from the balance of payments to the domestic money supply. The latter chain of causation is all the more likely the more highly specialised an economy is and, therefore, the less external stocks on the balance of payments tend to cancel out.
27. The 1974 balance-of-payments deficits of some industrialised countries of

the western world was partly due to the increase in the price of oil. The monetary theory of the balance of payments argues that the money market is the proper framework to analyse how this kind of disturbance is eliminated.

28. *Ex-post* flow measures were defined as $(\dot{m}^{*}_{i\cdot t} - \dot{m}_{i\cdot t})M_{i\cdot t}$.
29. *Ex post* excess demand for M_1 does not appear in Table 2.6, since it is not significant. However, excess demand for money of the rest of the world, defined *ex post*, is highly significant.
30. Courchene and Singh (1976) have estimated similar regressions on quarterly data for 14 countries, including Italy. They regress the balance of payments on a measure of *ex ante* excess demand for money, both for the individual countries and for the whole group; however, the specification of excess demand for money they use differs from that adopted here.
31. This change in the effect of domestic monetary aggregates on the balance of payments after the mid-1960s is confirmed by the direct tests of Section 1.
32. See, for instance, Blejer (1975) and Genberg (1975), Chapter 3. See also Knight and Wymer (1979). For a small-scale disequilibrium model of the Italian economy estimated in continuous time using Wymer's programmes, see Tullio (1980) and Chiesa (1979).

3 The Money Supply Process, Development of Financial Markets and Objectives of Italian Monetary Policy: 1960–78

INTRODUCTION

In Chapter 2 the change in the objectives of Italian monetary policy which occurred after the mid-1960s was briefly dealt with, and reaction functions of the Bank of Italy were estimated separately for the period prior to 1966 and for the period from 1966 to 1973 on quarterly data.

In this chapter the change in the objectives of Italian monetary policy during the 1960s will be analysed in greater detail in order to see to what extent the declared aims of official monetary policy were matched by *ex post* behaviour. A reaction function will also be estimated for the flexible exchange-rate period. Three periods will therefore be considered: from 1960[1] to 1965, from 1966 to 1973, and from 1974 to 1978.

The separation between the first two periods reflects the start of official interventions in the bond market by the Bank of Italy (Sartorelli, 1973) and the shift of the objectives of monetary policy toward shorter-run stabilisation of the level of economic activity (Savona, 1975). The separation is somewhat arbitrary, but it allows two distinct periods to be identified. The second period is characterised by much wider fluctuations in the balance of payments, which the results of the previous chapter suggest were closely connected with the behaviour of domestic assets of the Bank of Italy (see Figures 2 and 3 of Chapter 2). As far as the distinction between the second and the third periods is concerned, the degree of flexibility of the exchange rate provides the logic of the separation. Although the lira became flexible in 1973, the first major depreciation occurred in 1974.

This analysis (leaving aside the question of social and political tensions) aims to shed some light on the change in the behaviour and constraints of the monetary authorities and thus contribute to an understanding of the Italian balance-of-payments crises and higher rates of inflation.

In Section 1 the declared objectives of monetary policy in the various periods are briefly discussed. Given the importance of institutional aspects pertaining to the money supply process for understanding the behaviour of the monetary authorities, Section 2 will be devoted to an analysis of the money supply process in Italy. Section 3 contains an analysis of the main developments of financial markets during the 1960s and the 1970s. Section 4 contains a very brief survey of the literature on the reaction function, which is intended to clarify the choice of the dependent variables in the reaction function used. It also includes estimates of the latter for the three periods mentioned above. Concluding comments are set forth in Section 5.

The analysis of this chapter indicates that control over the domestic component of the base was lost in the second period as a result of the attempts to peg interest rates in the presence of large budget deficits and to achieve shorter-run stabilisation of the level of economic activity.[2] The analysis also suggests that the pegging itself was to a large extent self-defeating (due to the inflationary potential of large changes in the domestic component and the ensuing reduction in the demand for bonds by the private sector). It also indicates that while sterilisations of reserve changes were largely unsuccessful in the second period, with the advent of flexible exchange rates the Bank of Italy regained some capability to insulate the monetary base from reserve changes, a result consistent with *a priori* belief in the greater freedom provided by flexible rates.

1. THE SHIFT IN THE OBJECTIVES OF MONETARY POLICY

In the post-war period up to about the mid-1960s, Italian monetary policy was mainly geared toward the longer-run objectives of controlling the rate of inflation and achieving appropriate growth of foreign exchange reserves. The latter objective was clearly expressed by Paolo Baffi:[3]

> Economic development requires that the central bank should create the amount of liquidity which is necessary to sustain it. Convertibility

> and the growth of foreign trade connected with economic development requires that foreign assets be increased along with domestic assets. In order to satisfy the two requirements part of the additional liquidity will have to be generated through the foreign component of the base . . . , according to an upward trend at which monetary policy will aim (1968, p. 12).

The achievement of both these objectives was possible until about the mid-1960s because of the relatively moderate financing requirements of the Treasury.

In the Italian institutional framework it is difficult for the Bank of Italy to resist political pressures to finance a government budget deficit, so that when this began to increase and to become more erratic, the Bank of Italy to a large extent lost control of the domestic component of the base. An institutional aspect which was very important in this connection was that Italy had no developed market for short-term bonds; the short-term bonds issued were all public and were all absorbed by the Bank of Italy and the large commercial banks. (In 1970 the amount of short-term bonds outstanding was about 7 percent of the total stock of fixed-interest securities and about one half of it was in the portfolio of the central bank.)[4]

It follows that the public was subject to substantial losses on capital account when interest rates increased, and this explains why the monetary authorities were extremely reluctant to let yields rise. The scope for sales of bonds to the public was therefore always extremely small whenever the budget deficit and inflationary expectations started to rise. A technical device adopted on more than one occasion by the Bank of Italy to try to avoid the increase in interest rates on securities was to impose controls on the portfolio composition of commercial banks, thus shifting upwards the overall demand for bonds. However, since the budget deficit was not promptly reduced once the banks had purchased the imposed quantity of bonds, the Bank of Italy had to intervene directly and the real solution to the problem was only postponed.

The larger fluctuations of the Treasury financing requirement after 1965 are explained partly by government attempts to reduce short-run fluctuations of the level of economic activity, partly by large expenditure programmes implemented by more socially oriented governments in the presence of increasing (or at least not decreasing) inefficiency in the public sector, and partly by the reduced political strength of governments unwilling or unable to finance at least part of the increased expenditure by taxation. A final factor may have been the dying-out of an older generation of economists and politicians raised in a tradition more hostile to high budget deficits.

After the introduction of flexible exchange rates, the Treasury financing requirement continued to increase more or less steadily and it remained the major constraint on the Bank of Italy's management of the monetary base, as in the previous period. However, particularly after 1976, the interest rate policy became much more flexible, thus allowing the Treasury to finance a substantially larger fraction of its deficit by selling Treasury bills and bonds to the public. The Bank of Italy could therefore improve its control over the creation of the domestic component of the monetary base, and the larger balance-of-payments surpluses of 1977 and 1978, which occurred despite the increasing public-sector borrowing requirement, are to a large extent not unrelated to this change in interest-rate policy. In addition to a greater control over the domestic component of the base, due to the flexible interest-rate policy, managed exchange rates also enhanced the possibility of insulating the total monetary base from foreign influences, as shown by the fact that sterilisation policies were successful in the 1974–8 period,[5] as opposed to the earlier period. Thanks to the freedom provided by greater flexibility of interest and exchange rates the Bank of Italy was once again in a position to pursue the objective of a growth of foreign reserves (expressed by Paolo Baffi above).[6]

It is evident from the preceding discussion that a proper understanding of the way the Italian monetary authorities have tried to achieve their objectives calls for an analysis of the money supply process, as well as of the structure of the Italian financial market and its developments over the last two decades. The next two sections (Sections 2 and 3) will therefore be devoted to each of these two topics. The estimates of the reaction function will be presented in Section 4.

2. THE MONEY SUPPLY PROCESS IN ITALY

During the post-war period the Italian monetary authorities have relied for control of monetary and credit aggregates on a variety of instruments in addition to the classical ones (i.e. the discount mechanism, changes in reserve requirements, and open-market operations). The use of these additional instruments, as well as of the classical tools of monetary control, has changed considerably over the last two decades. On the whole during the 1960s, mainly as a result of the relatively underdeveloped stage of the Italian money market, open-market operations on long-term bonds were performed more in order to peg interest rates (on long-term bonds) than as a means of controlling monetary aggregates – although the pegging had obvious side-effects on the monetary base. The use of the discount mechanism has been characterised by a high degree of discretion on the part of the Bank of Italy, although in the 1970s the role of the cost of financing from the central bank has been enhanced, both by gradually increasing the cost to banks in relation to the frequency of re-financing and by adjusting the basic discount rate to money market interest rates more frequently. As far as the role of reserve requirements is concerned, until the reform of 1975 commercial bank assets at the central bank, as well as particular types of Treasury bills and bonds (both private and public), were allowed for inclusion among required reserves.[7] It followed that reserve requirements could not be clearly separated as an instrument of monetary control from selective credit policies aimed at easing the flow of credit to particular sectors of the economy.

In addition to the standard classical ones, the instruments most frequently used were: direct control of the net foreign asset position of commercial banks, compulsory purchases of bonds by commercial banks (*vincoli di portafoglio*), and ceilings on bank loans in lire (*massimali sugli impieghi bancari*). While the control of the net foreign asset position of commercial banks was frequently used during the 1960s (for example, during the 1963–4 balance-of-payments crisis) and remained important in the 1970s, direct credit controls were introduced on a large scale only in 1973 and thereafter were intensified or relaxed largely in relation to balance-of-payments and exchange-rate developments. Since 1977–8 the policy of the Bank of Italy has been to move away from direct credit controls. At present (mid-1979) compulsory bond purchases have been to a large extent phased out. Largely because of the development of a money market, albeit a still rudimentary one,[8] and the 1975 reform of the reserve requirement mechanism which has made the instrument much more flexible, the Bank of Italy is now in a better position to control monetary aggregates without recourse to direct credit controls, which interfere with the efficiency of the banking system, are cumbersome to administer, distort the allocation of credit, and are to a large extent unpredictable as far as their affect on monetary and credit aggregates is concerned, because of loopholes which are difficult to eliminate.

A further expedient which was used on two occasions during severe balance-of-payments and exchange-rate crises (1974, 1976) to control the monetary base and the money supply was a compulsory three-months, 50 percent, non-interest-bearing deposit on purchases of foreign exchange. The deposit was held at the Bank of Italy and amounted to a sterilisation of the monetary base during the three-month period.

Before analysing in more detail the instruments of control of monetary aggregates in Italy, it is important to note that during the 1960s and the 1970s the prevailing view in Italy has been that the control of credit is more important than the control of money for stabilisation purposes, and that while long-term credit granted by financial intermediaries to firms heavily influences investment, bank credit has a strong effect on inventory accumulation. However, the opposite view that money matters more than credit and that the ultimate use of funds by firms cannot be linked too strictly to the sources of the funds (self-financing, long-term or short-term funds), which is generally more in line with the approach adopted in this book to analysing and explaining balance-of-payments and exchange-rate developments, also has followers within the Bank of Italy itself.

A. The discount mechanism

Re-financing by commercial banks from the Bank of Italy became less important in the early 1970s in connection with the increased liquidity injected into the system through other channels, in particular through the increase in the public-sector borrowing requirement. In addition, interest rates on loans by the Bank of Italy have been adjusted more frequently to money market rates, thus reducing the price incentive to borrow which had often existed previously. Also, the recent development of a money market has reduced the importance of this source of monetary-base creation, although the latter's variability has increased because of the wider fluctuations of the public-sector borrowing requirement, the introduction and phasing-out of compulsory deposits on purchases of foreign exchange, and the existence of direct credit controls.

B. Constraints on the net foreign asset position of commercial banks

The Bank of Italy has control over the net foreign asset position of commercial banks. It can compel commercial banks to reach a zero, or a specified negative or positive net foreign asset position within a certain period of time. For example, by demanding that commercial banks increase their net foreign asset position, reserve inflows can be kept smaller or outflows larger. Thus, the monetary base can be controlled through the foreign channel. Incentives like swap agreements often accompanied the directives in the 1960s, particularly when a reduction in the expansion of liquidity arising from balance-of-payments surpluses seemed to be called for. In the 1970s the power to control directly the net foreign asset position of commercial banks has, in general, not been used. However, the net foreign asset position was heavily influenced by the ceilings on the expansion of bank loans introduced in 1973, from which bank loans in foreign exchange were exempted. The ceilings, by exempting bank loans in foreign exchange, represented a strong incentive for banks to borrow abroad and lend to domestic firms in foreign exchange, thus helping to redress the balance of payments and to strengthen the lira relatively quickly (for example, during 1976–7). On the whole, especially in the latter period, also changes in interest-rate differentials played an important role in determining the net foreign asset position.[9]

C. Reserve requirements of commercial banks and compulsory bond purchases

As stated above, until 1975 reserve requirements overlapped as an instrument of monetary control with selective credit policies, due to the inclusion among required reserves of particular types of fixed-interest securities. The 1975 reform established that only deposits at the central bank could be considered as reserves and therefore separated the reserve requirement machanism from compulsory bond purchases. Reserve requirements were also made uniform across banks and for different types of deposits, and were set as a ratio of the *flow* of new deposits instead of the existing *stock* of deposits. Thus, the mechanism became much more flexible. The Governor of the Bank of Italy was empowered to change the required reserve ratio between 10 percent and 20 percent and the interest rate paid on required reserves held by banks. The latter faculty constitutes an additional tool of monetary policy since it enables the Bank of Italy to affect the overall profit position of commercial banks.

Compulsory purchases of bonds were imposed on commercial banks in 1965 as a measure of selective credit policy. In June 1973, during a period of accelerating inflation, increased public-sector borrowing requirement and a worsening balance of payments, the demand for bonds by the public and commercial banks was weakening. In order to sustain the demand for bonds and at the same time avoid a rise in interest rates, the monetary authorities laid down that by the end of the year commercial banks should hold in their portfolios bonds equivalent to at least 6 percent of the stock of total deposits held at the end of 1972. The measure was accompanied by selective credit-policy measures, insofar as some types of bond were favoured more than others. The measure had the effect of reducing the fraction of the public-sector borrowing requirement financed by monetary-base creation (for given interest rates). However, as the public-sector borrowing requirement kept increasing, the measure was not sufficient to stop the increase in the monetary base. As was to be expected, since the main factors affecting the excess supply of bonds (namely, the reduction in real interest rates and the increase in the public-sector borrowing requirement) were not corrected,[10] the need to make the requirement more stringent was soon felt and by the end of 1974 the ratio of required bond purchases to deposits had been raised twice.

D. Open-market operations and the development of the money market

In the 1960s and the early 1970s, when the Treasury bills in circulation were a small fraction of total fixed-interest security, open-market operations were mainly in long-term bonds. Purchases and sales by the Bank of Italy, however, were aimed more at the pegging of interest rates (especially from 1966 to 1969 and from 1973 to mid-1974) than at the management of the monetary base. By 1976 Treasury bills in circulation had become 29 percent of total fixed-interest securities (as opposed to 7 percent in 1970), and purchases and sales of Treasury bills for the purpose of managing the monetary base had become more common. This widespread use of Treasury bills as a means of financing the budget deficit arose from the crisis in the bond market, the acceleration of inflation, and the Treasury's reluctance to commit itself to fixing high nominal interest rates on newly issued long-term bonds, when inflation might be hoped to slow down.

The Italian money market is still in a rudimentary stage because there is basically only one supplier of short-term instruments (the Treasury), the secondary market in Treasury bills still lacks depth, breadth and resilience, and because the payment of competitive interest rates on current and savings accounts discourages demand of money market assets. Nevertheless, the Bank of Italy is nowadays in a position to exercise more control over the growth of the monetary base of the Treasury and hence to achieve more efficiently the level of bank reserves at which the Bank is aiming.

3. MAIN DEVELOPMENTS IN ITALIAN FINANCIAL MARKETS: 1960–78

The purpose of this section is to sketch the main developments in Italian financial markets in the course of the 1960s and in particular of the 1970s. Since developments in the 1970s especially have been closely dependent on the interest-rate policy pursued by the authorities in the face of increasing budget deficits, and increased direct intervention by the authorities in the composition of banks' portfolios, particular attention will be devoted to the latter two topics. The trend towards intervention in commercial banks' portfolios was reversed in 1977 and 1978, as the authorities adopted a policy of adjusting nominal interest rates to inflation more promptly. However, the Government itself has increasingly taken on the role of financial intermediator.

A. Trends and fluctuations in the size of the bond market

In relation to GDP, the Italian bond market has for some considerable time been higher than in countries such as France and Germany. As Figure 3.1 shows, during the 1970s the fraction of total net issues to GDP remained higher in Italy than in Germany and France. The size of the Italian bond market, at least in part, reflects the relatively smaller scale of the stock market. The figure also shows that the ratio displayed a positive trend, as in Germany, but unlike in France, and that fluctuations around the trend were much greater than in the other two countries.

The increasing size of the Italian bond market in relation to GDP was largely due to increased issues of bonds by the enlarged public sector, which was itself a consequence of the increased public-sector borrowing requirements. Figure 3.2 shows that the net issues of bonds by the government sector as a fraction of total net issues increased from below 40 percent in the early 1970s to almost 80 percent in 1978. The fall in the share of bonds issued by others (enterprises and special credit institutions) was accompanied by a considerable profit squeeze, largely connected with increases in real wages. Enterprises were therefore crowded out[11] of the bond market and had to rely more heavily on short-term financing, particularly bank credit, and government transfers. Gross government transfers to enterprises were about 11,500 billion lira in 1978 (or 5.8 percent of GDP) and are expected to go up further. This increasing role of the government budget deficit as financial intermediator represents a distortion in the flow of funds and also a loosening of the responsibilities connected with the lending of funds.[12]

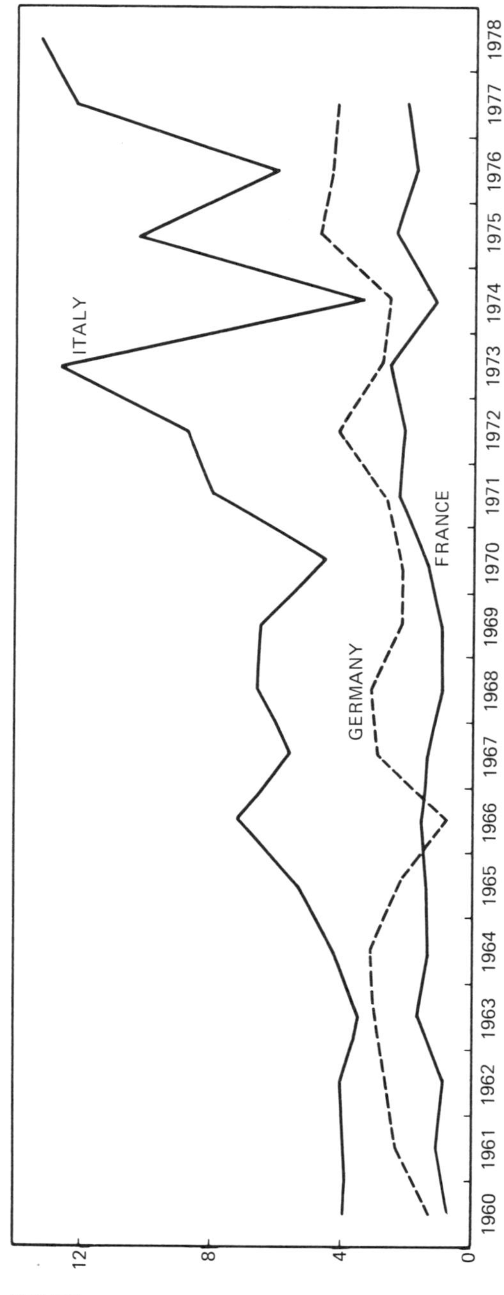

Source: OECD and Bank of Italy

Fig. 3.1 Total net issues of bonds as a fraction of GDP

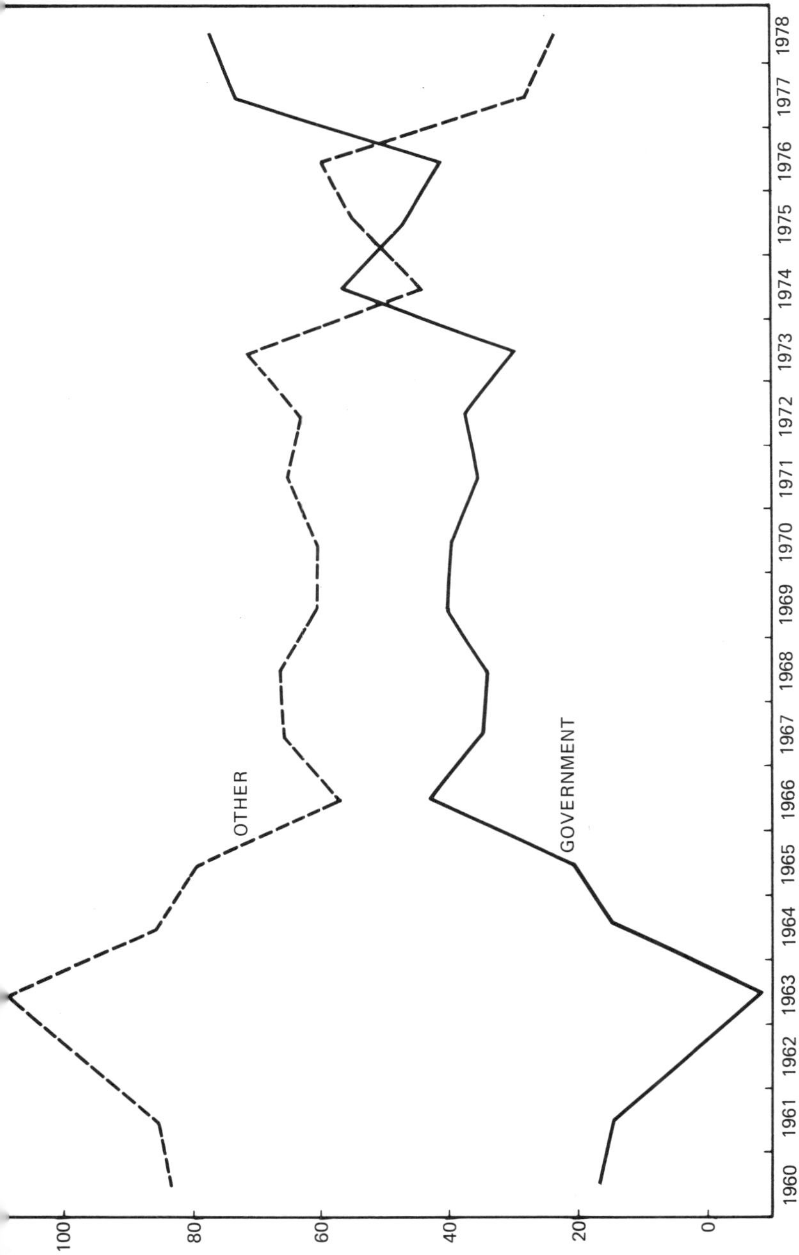

Source: OECD

Fig. 3.2 Net issues of bonds by supplier (as percentage of total issues)

The larger fluctuations in the fraction of net issues to GDP observed for Italy in the 1970s can be explained by the fact that the Bank of Italy controls the issues of securities by means of authorisation. When it feels that the market will not be able to absorb new issues, authorisations are withheld in order to avoid unwanted expansions of the monetary base through purchases of bonds by the Bank. (For instance, the years 1974 and 1976 were years in which rising inflationary expectations led households and enterprises to abstain from the purchase of new bonds, and even to sell bonds that were already in their portfolios.) This leads us to consider in the next section the determinants of the demand for bonds by the public.

B. Demand for bonds by households and enterprises

Figure 3.3 compares the bonds purchased by households and firms[13] as a fraction of GDP and a proxy for the real interest rate on government bonds. The correlation between the two time series is quite high. Thus, the dramatic fall in real interest rates in 1973, 1974 and 1976 explains to a considerable extent the crisis of the Italian bond market in those years.

Adjustments of nominal interest rates to rising inflationary expectations were delayed in 1973 for a number of reasons. Firstly, an investment boom was under way and the Bank of Italy did not want to take the responsibility of halting it. Secondly, because of the relatively large amount of bonds in the public's portfolio and their relatively long average time to maturity, the public suffers large capital losses when nominal interest rates are increased. Thus, increases in nominal rates are believed to discourage investment in the bond market. Finally, nominal interest rates were not adjusted to minimise the interest burden of the Treasury. Italian monetary authorities reacted in 1973 to the unwillingness of the public to purchase bonds, first by compelling commercial banks to purchase bonds (June 1973)[14] and, second, by starting issuing larger amounts of Treasury bills and encouraging the participation of nonbank financial intermediaries to the bills auction.

Thus, the fraction of total bond issues purchased by commercial banks and by the Bank of Italy increased dramatically in 1974, and again in 1976 when the major crisis of the lira occurred.

Treasury bills were traditionally absorbed largely by commercial banks and by the Bank of Italy. In 1976 total issues were about 25 percent of total issues of fixed-interest securities, as opposed to 7 percent in 1970. From 1975, following the sharp increase in the real interest rate paid on them, private and institutional investment in Treasury bills became increasingly popular (Figure 3.4).

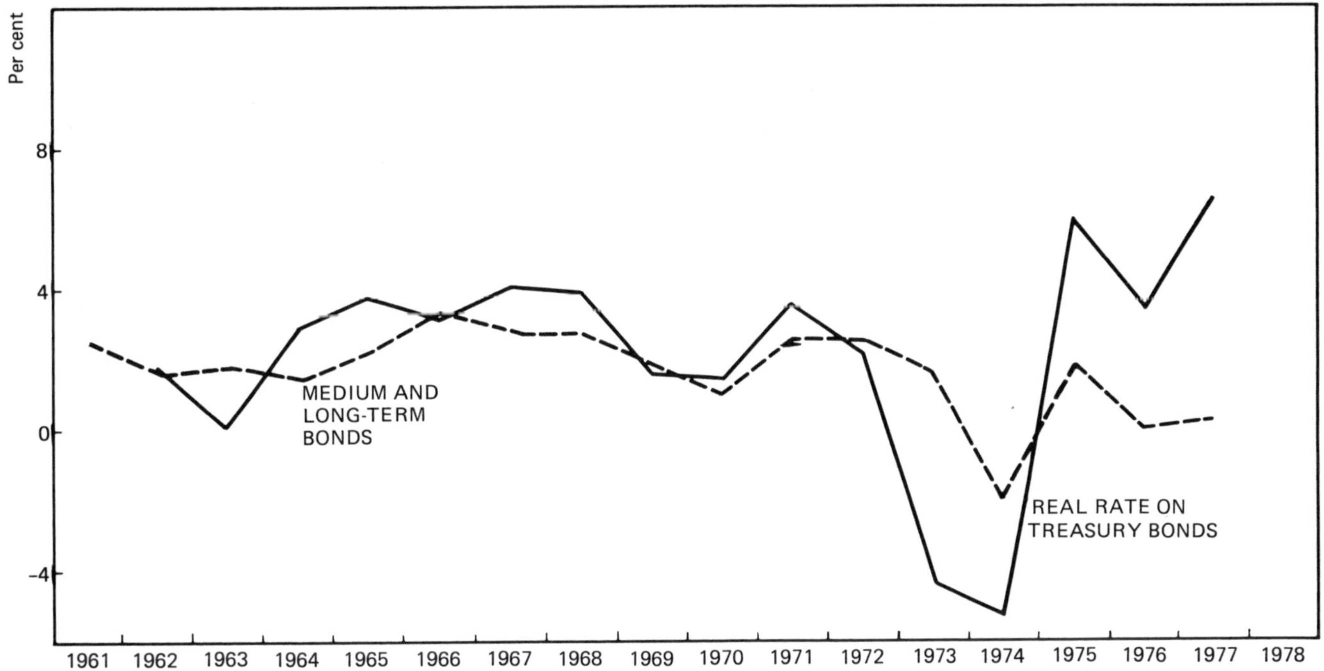

Source: Bank of Italy
* Includes purchases by insurance companies, special credit institution and pension funds.
† Expected rate of inflation calculated by Bank of Italy on the basis of semi-annual surveys.

Fig 3.3 Medium-and long-term bonds purchased by households and enterprises as a fraction of GDP and real interest rate on Treasury bonds†*

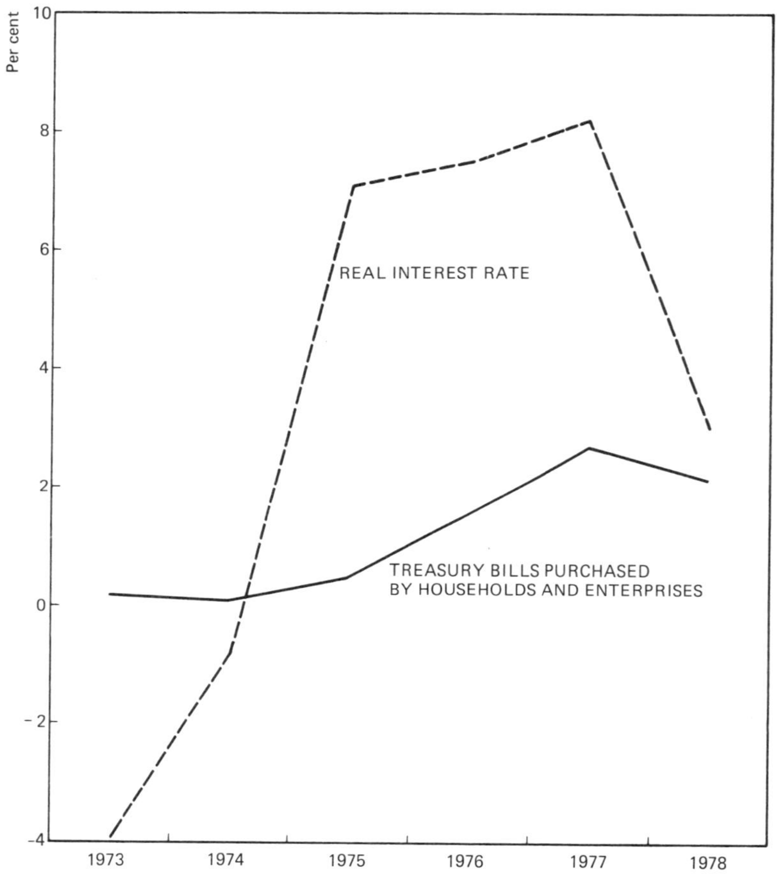

* Includes purchases by insurance companies, special credit institutions and pension funds.

† Expected rate of inflation calculated by the Bank of Italy on the basis of semi-annual surveys.

Fig. 3.4 Treasury bills purchased by households and enterprises as a fraction of GDP and real interest rate on Treasury bills†*

4. REACTION FUNCTION OF THE ITALIAN MONETARY AUTHORITIES (1960–5, 1966–73, 1974–8)

In the existing literature on the reaction function[15] there is no general agreement as to the specific form of the target variable representing the external transaction goal, nor as to which variable representing the overall thrust of monetary policy should be used as the dependent variable. Interest rates, the money supply, the total monetary base, unborrowed reserves, and the domestic component of the base have been used as the dependent variable.

Following Ujiie (1975) the domestic component of the base will be used, since for a relatively small open economy it is the true policy variable of the system and the only variable among the ones mentioned above which the monetary authorities (i.e. the Bank of Italy and the Government) can control under fixed exchange rates. Since the price level and the interest rate of a small country with fixed exchange rates are determined – except in the short run – by the rest of the world, the monetary theory of the balance of payments considers the money stock, the total monetary base, and interest rates as variables outside the control of the monetary authorities. Although the monetary authorities of a small country might consider the total money supply or interest rates or the total monetary base as magnitudes under their control, changes in the domestic component of the base must reflect, *ex post*, the overall thrust of monetary policy (Ujiie, 1975).

For a large country like the United States, on the other hand, it is reasonable to consider the total monetary base as the proper monetary policy indicator, since the United States is a reserve currency country with – since 1971 – an inconvertible gold stock.

The other monetary policy indicator mentioned above (unborrowed reserves) is too much affected by demand conditions (for unborrowed reserves), and therefore should not be used as the dependent variable in reaction functions. This is true for both large and small countries.

The target variable representing the external transaction goal most used in the literature is the balance of payments. This reflects central bank neutralisation policies but not the external transaction goal which Baffi refers to above (see p. 58). Ujiie (1975) has shown in a formal model of a small open economy that the target variable which should be included in the reaction function for the external transaction goal is the level of reserves. In the empirical tests, therefore, the external transaction goal will be represented by the level of reserves.

The reaction function estimated separately for the three periods (1960–II to 1965–IV; 1966–I to 1973–IV; 1974–I to 1978–IV) has the following form:

$$\mathrm{d}DA = \beta_1 TFR + \beta_2 \mathrm{d}r_F + \beta_3(NIR^* - NIR) + \beta_4(\dot{P} - \dot{P}^*) + \beta_5(u - u^*) + \beta_6 \mathrm{d}IIP + \beta_7 B$$

where the expected signs are: $\beta_1, \beta_3, \beta_4, \beta_6, \beta_7 < 0$ and $\beta_2, \beta_5 > 0$ and where DA is the domestic assets of the Bank of Italy. The other symbols have the following meaning:

TFR	= the Treasury financing requirements, defined as revenue minus expenditure;
$r_F = r$	= the interest rate on bonds issued by financing institutions (*instituti di credito mobiliare*);
NIR	= the net foreign position of the Bank of Italy and the Italian Exchange Office;
NIR_t^*	= the ten-quarter average of $NIR_t \ldots NIR_{t-9}$;
$\dot{p}$	= the rate of change of the consumer price index; $\dot{p}^*$, the desired rate of inflation, is put equal to zero for simplicity;
u, u^*	= the actual and desired unemployment rates; the desired unemployment rate has been assumed equal to 3 percent throughout;
IIP	= the index of industrial production;
B	= the balance of payments;
d	always indicates a first difference and a dot a percentage change.

The data were obtained from the Bank of Italy and ISCO publications and from the *International Financial Statistics* of the International Monetary Fund.

The interest rates on bonds issued by financial institutions were preferred to those on government bonds; because the Bank of Italy pegged the latter more heavily in the second period, they often fail to reflect the overall market pressure on interest rates.

NIR was lagged one period in order to avoid reverse causation problems between dDA and NIR, since when DA increases sharply NIR goes down in the same quarter. Reverse causation is not eliminated by lagging NIR if the public anticipates changes in DA, but it is unlikely that such anticipations are important enough to bias the coefficient of $(NIR^* - NIR_{-1})$in the reaction function. Changes in nominal or real income were not included in the regressions in order to avoid reverse causation problems.

The index of industrial production was included in order to assess to what extent the objective, pursued in the second period, of stabilising economic activity was achieved, and the rate of inflation in order to assess the extent to which the inflation objective was achieved. The unemployment rate should measure the employment objective and the balance of payments the neutralisation objective. The variable representing the unemployment objective $(u - u^*)$ was never significant. Rates of capacity utilisation were substituted for the rate of unemployment but with no success. The variable representing the inflation target also was never significant.

The specification of the reaction function adopted suffers from several shortcomings. In the first place, in the latter part of the second period exchange rates were no longer fixed and this might have changed the behaviour of the Italian monetary authorities. However, the period of floating was restricted to 1973 when heavy interventions in the foreign exchange market also occurred. In 1973 the objective of pegging interest rates had not been abandoned and the policy of financing a large fraction of the Treasury financing requirement, which as will be seen below was the most important explanatory variable in the reaction function, had not been discontinued. It was therefore decided to leave the year 1973 in the sample period without changing the specification adopted of the reaction function. As far as the third period is concerned, the rate of change of the effective exchange rate was added to the explanatory variable to check whether a systematic stabilisation target of the exchange rate could be detected.

A second problem arises from the fact that dDA is the dependent variable in accordance with the small-country assumption of the monetary approach, which implies that, if exchange rates are fixed, dr_F, $\dot{p}$ and $\dot{p}^*$ are not under the control of the small country. Although fixed exchange rates imply that in the long run this is true, it has been argued in Chapter 2 that the Italian price level, the rate of inflation, and the interest rate can be different (and were, in fact, different) from those in other countries for periods certainly longer than a quarter. The inclusion of dr_F and ($\dot{p}$ and $\dot{p}^*$) reflects, therefore, the fact that the real world departs from the steady-state assumption and that Italian monetary authorities might want to keep them for some time at levels which are not compatible with the maintenance of fixed exchange rates if the objective is maintained for longer periods of time, or that they might want to bring them back into line with foreign variables, once they have departed from them for too long.

On the whole, the most important variables in the reaction function are the Treasury financing requirement, the interest rate, and seasonal dummy variables. The growth of the reserves target $(NIR^* - NIR_{-1})$ and the economic activity target $(dIIP)$ played a role in the first and the third period. The sign of $dIIP$ was, however, positive, implying that a policy of accommodating activity changes was followed. As far as the

*Table 3.1 Reaction function of Italian monetary authorities: changes in domestic assets of the Bank of Italy. Quarterly data**

No. of regr.	Sample period	NIR^*-NIR_{-1}	TFR	dr	dIIP	D_1	D_3	D_4	D_{63}†	B	R^2 / DW	$SER/\bar{x}$
1	1960–II	−0·23	−0·31	326·7	14·7	−200	−145	254	142	–	0·90	0·57
	to	(−1·68)	(−2·0)	(2·95)	(0·63)	(−2·57)	(−1·66)	(2·89)	(2·32)		1·80	
			−0·26	238·5	36·6	−285	−180	291	182	−0.19	0.89	0.69
2	1965–IV		(−1·64)	(1·90)	(1·68)	(−4·20)	(−1·91)	(3·27)	(3·30)	(−1·04)	1·50	
3	1966–I	−0·05	−0·81	492·4	14·4	−839	−764	–	–	–	0·81	0·57
	to	(−0·37)	(−7·60)	(2·25)	(0·62)	(−5·50)	(−4·83)				1·81	
		–	−0·79	426·7	11·7	−841	−746	–	–	−0·15	0·81	0·57
4	1973–IV		(−8·17)	(1·81)	(0·50)	(−5·56)	(−4·70)			(−0·78)	1·87	
5	1974–I	−0·35	−0·15	1471·2	171·9	498	−240	–	–	–	0·57	0·83
	to	(−1·71)	(−1·67)	(3·09)	(1·69)	(0·54)	(−0·26)				0·93	
		−0·25	−0·37	730·3	180·4	−986	106	–	–	−1·03	0·75	0·66
6	1978–IV	(−1·51)	(−3·65)	(1·63)	(2·23)	(−1·13)	(0·14)			(−3·06)	1·58	

Sources: Bank of Italy; IMF, *International Financial Statistics*.

* Source of dependent variable: line 12a plus 12e of *IFS*.

† D_{63} assumes the value of plus one for the four quarters of 1963 and the first quarter of 1964 and zero otherwise. It reflects the wage push during 1963/4.

‡ $\bar{x}$ indicates the average of the absolute values of the dependent variable. It is about 190 billion lire in the first period, 690 billion lire in the second and 2100 billion lire in the third.

success of the neutralisation objective is concerned the evidence is clear: only after the introduction of a managed float system were the Italian monetary authorities able to neutralise fully the effect of foreign reserve changes on the total monetary bases.

Table 3.1 contains regressions of the domestic component of the monetary base on target variables of monetary policy. D_i is a dummy variable referring to quarter *i (1* = first quarter of the year, 4 = fourth quarter). Numbers in parentheses indicate $t-$statistics.[16]

The target variable representing the economic activity stabilisation objectives was significant during the first and the third period. In the first and the third period domestic assets fluctuated pro-cyclically.[17] The coefficient of *TFR* is substantially larger and much more significant in the second than in the first period.[18] It loses significance during the flexible exchange-rate period, when interest-rate policy became much more flexible, particularly in 1977 and 1978.

There is also evidence that, at least for quarterly time intervals, the Bank of Italy reacted in all three periods to increases in interest rates by pumping liquidity into the system and vice versa. As far as the third period is concerned, the rate of change of the exchange rate did not have a significant coefficient. The dummy variables for the first and fourth quarter of the year reflect the well-known expansion of the domestic component of the base in the fourth quarter and its contraction in the succeeding quarter. Similarly, the dummy for the third quarter reflects the seasonal expansion of the foreign component of the base and the accompanying contraction of the domestic component.

*Table 3.2 Reaction function of Italian monetary authorities: changes in claims on Government. Quarterly data**

No. of regr.	Sample period	*TFR*	d*IIP*	*B*	R^2	DW	$\frac{SER}{\bar{x}}$	$\bar{x}$
7	1960–II to 1965–IV	−0·56 (−6·60)	–	–	0·61	1·6	0·77	152·79
8	1966–I to 1973–IV	−0·47 (−8·79)	–	–	0·55	1·4	0·76	438·83
9	1974–I to 1978–IV	−0·35 (−4·30)	261·52 (3·19)	−0·91 (−3·21)	0·61	1·6	0·71	2172·86

Sources: Bank of Italy; IMF, *International Financial Statistics.*

* Source of dependent variable: line 12a of *IFS*.

*Table 3.3 Reaction function of Italian monetary authorities: changes in claims on commercial banks. Quarterly data**

No. of *regr.*	Sample *period*	d*IIP*	d*r*	D_1	D_3	D_4	*B*	R^2 DW	$\frac{SER}{\bar{x}}$	$\bar{x}$	ρ
	1960–II	93·6	335·9	−206	−141·0	30	−0·28	0·88			
10	to								0·49	126·77	−0·51
	1965–IV	(8·41)	(5·13)	(6·08)	(−3·46)	(1·03)	(−3·37)	2·0			
	1966–I	29·9	214·3	−572	−521	791	−0·05	0·63			
11	to								0·84	567·0	–
	1873–IV	(1·07)	(0·78)	(−3·15)	(−3·04)	(4·57)	(−0·25)	2·3			
	1974–I	−80·22	340·0	−153	−631	−55	0·04	0·41			
12	to								1·09	650·00	–
	1978–IV	(−2·01)	(1·64)	(−0·45)	(−1·67)	(−0·15)	(0·29)	2·3			

Sources: Bank of Italy; IMF, *International Financial Statistics*.
* Source of dependent variable: line 12e of *IFS*.

In Table 3.2 and 3.3 the domestic component of the base as defined in Table 3.1 is split into its two components (claims on the government and claims on the banks).

In neither of the three periods did the Treasury monetary base react in a significant way to interest-rate changes, to the index of industrial production, or to ($NIR^* - NIR_{-1}$). In addition to the progressive fall of the coefficient of *TFR*, the table shows that in the third period when the Treasury component of the monetary base became a very large fraction of the total monetary base, expansions in activity were accommodated via changes in the claims on the government, as opposed to the early 1960s when claims on banks changed for that purpose (cf. Regression 10 of Table 3.3). Also reserve changes were neutralised via changes in the claims on government during the most recent period.

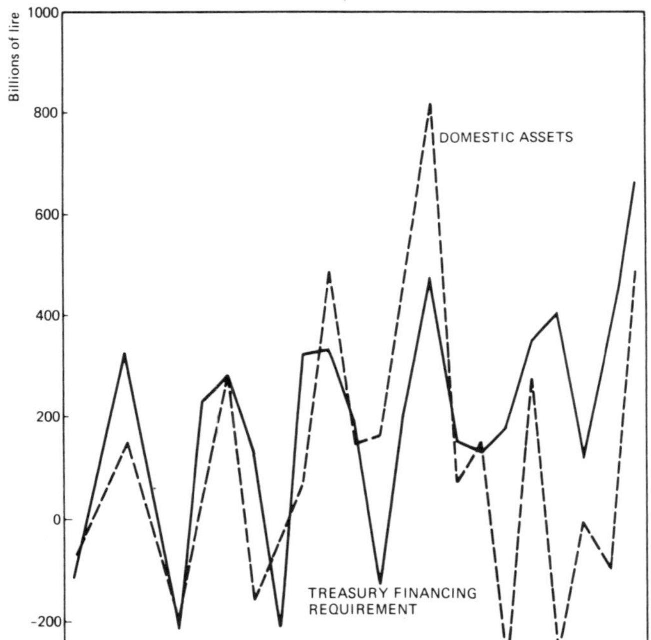

Source: Bank of Italy

Fig. 3.5 Quarterly changes in domestic assets of the Bank of Italy and Treasury financing requirement (1960–5)

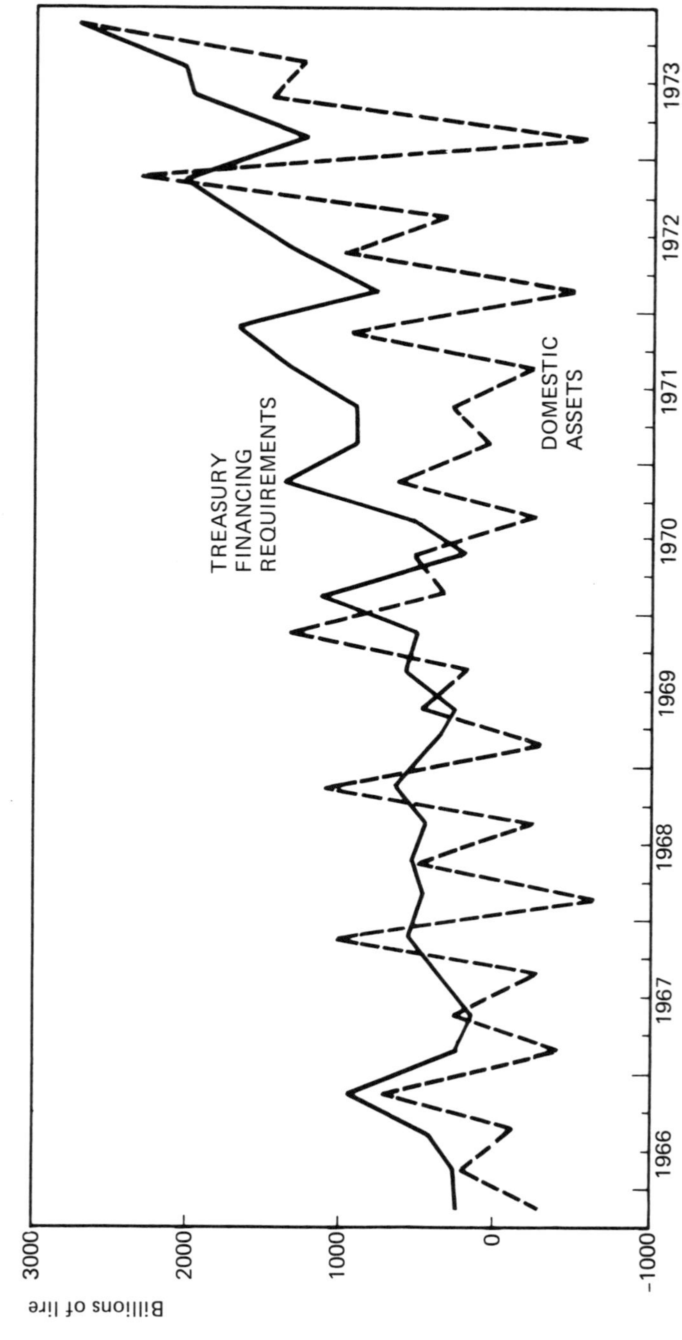

Source: Bank of Italy

Fig. 3.6 Quarterly changes in domestic assets of the Bank of Italy and Treasury financing requirement (1966–73)

Table 3.3 shows that the Bank of Italy pursued the objectives of pegging interest rates by manipulating the monetary base of the commercial banks. Changes in the level of economic activity were accommodated via changes in the claims on banks in the first period. In the third period the regression has a very low explanatory power, probably because claims on banks became a small and insignificant fraction of the total monetary base. The negative and significant sign of the coefficient of D_3 indicates that the reserve inflows of the third quarter were largely neutralised in all three periods.[19]

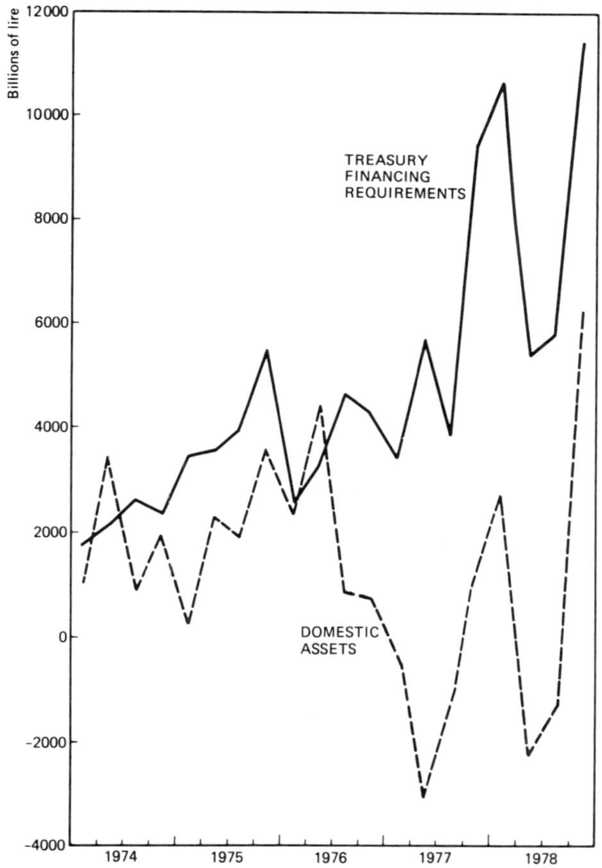

Source: Bank of Italy

Fig. 3.7 Quarterly changes in domestic assets of the Bank of Italy and Treasury financing requirements (1974–8)

Figures 3.5, 3.6 and 3.7 below show the changes in domestic assets of the Bank of Italy and the Treasury financing requirement.[20] They reveal that during the first half of the 1960s changes in domestic assets bore a high correlation to the Treasury financing requirement, but that fluctuations were on the whole within narrow margins and periods of increases both in domestic assets and the Treasury financing requirement were followed by periods of reductions in both aggregates (Figure 3.5). In the succeeding period the Treasury financing requirement was never negative and was subject to a strong upward trend. The correlation between the two aggregates was still high but less pronounced than in the previous period. In the 1974–8 period, and especially in 1977–8, with the pursuit of a much more flexible interest-rate policy, domestic assets no longer followed particularly closely the behaviour of the Treasury financing requirement, as evidenced also by the regressions, despite the fact that the latter reached unprecedented levels.

5. CONCLUSIONS

In this chapter we have first of all described the main instruments of monetary control in Italy during the 1960s and 1970s, and the main developments in Italian financial markets. We then presented rough estimates of a reaction function of the Italian monetary authorities separately for the periods 1960–5, 1966–73, and 1974–8 on quarterly data. The reaction function estimated suffers from a number of shortcomings. First of all, to avoid a simultaneous equation bias the reaction functions should be estimated within the context of a full macro-economic model (Bergstrom and Wymer, 1976; Jonson, 1976; Sanssapour and Sheen, 1976; and Knight and Wymer, 1979). However, this lies outside the scope of this chapter whose main aim has been to show the dependence of domestic monetary growth on the Treasury financing requirement and the constraints the Treasury has imposed on the Bank of Italy. Secondly, the dependent variable in the reaction function might better be expressed in terms of rates of change or accelerations.[21] But since the focus of this book is on the balance of payments consistency demanded that the former be related to absolute changes in domestic assets of the central bank.[22] Nevertheless, the regressions suggest the following conclusions:

1. The pegging of interest rates was no more effective in the late 1960s than in the early years of the decade, despite official intentions, since, if the coefficients of the interest rate are corrected for the different average

absolute value of the changes in domestic assets, the coefficient is much smaller in the second part of the 1960s than previously.

2. With the adoption of a more flexible interest-rate policy after April 1974 the close link between the changes in the domestic assets of the Bank of Italy and the Treasury financing requirement was finally broken.[23] Although the link had also been very close in the early part of the 1960s, there were no major negative effects at the time, because the Treasury financing requirement fluctuated between much narrower margins and did not show a strong positive trend.

3. The objective of the accumulation of foreign exchange reserves could be pursued only in the first and the third periods. It was crowded out in the second period.

4. Full sterilisation of foreign reserve inflows and outflows was possible only during the flexible exchange-rate period. No strong and significant sterilisation could be detected from 1960 to 1973. However, seasonal foreign reserve inflows in the third quarter of each year, connected with revenues from tourism, were sterilised successfully during all three periods.

5. The stabilisation of interest rates and the accommodation to changes in activity were pursued by manipulating the claims on the commercial banks during the fixed exchange-rate period. After 1974 claims on commercial banks became such a small fraction of the total domestic claims of the Bank of Italy that they seem to have lost their former importance.

The analysis developed focused on the shift in the objectives of Italian monetary policy. It showed that the interventions in the bond market by the Bank of Italy in the 1966–73 period caused it to lose control of the changes in the domestic component of the monetary base, which became largely dependent on the wider fluctuations of the Treasury financing requirement.

If one accepts the view expressed by the proponents of the monetary approach to balance-of-payments theory, that a high rate of expansion of the domestic source component of the base, compared with the average rate of the corresponding variable of the main trading partners' countries, is relevant to balance-of-payments developments (or alternatively, if exchange rates are flexible, to exchange-rate developments), the shift in the objectives of Italian monetary policy in the presence of much larger and more erratic changes in the Treasury financing requirement, contributes to an explanation of recent Italian payments crises.

The choice of a nominal interest-rate stabilisation target instead of a target representing an appropriate range of rates of change of the domestic assets of the central bank, or a real interest-rate target, was a factor in the loss of control over the domestic rate of inflation. In 1977 and 1978, however, a move was made toward the stabilisation of real instead of nominal rates.

NOTES TO CHAPTER 3

1. The choice of the initial quarter is determined by the availability of quarterly data.
2. Recent theoretical developments in the field of balance-of-payments theory (Mundell, 1968, 1971; Johnson, 1973) imply that control of the domestic component of the base is of paramount importance in avoiding large fluctuations in the overall balance of payments. The tests of the Italian balance of payments presented in the previous chapter strongly support this view. This chapter is therefore highly complementary with Chapter 2. See, in particular, Section 1 of Chapter 2, where balance-of-payments equations and reaction functions are tested simultaneously.
3. Governor of the Bank of Italy since 1975 and General Manager of the Bank from 1960 to 1975.
4. Short-term Treasury bills have, however, become an important instrument to finance government budget deficits since 1973. See Section 3.
5. See Regression 6 of Table 3.1 and Regression 9 of Table 3.2
6. See Regression 5 and 6, Table 3.1
7. The types of assets which could be included were changed from time to time.
8. See Section 3.
9. Contrary to the official method of defining the balance of payments, capital movements of commercial banks have therefore been put above the balance-of-payments line and considered as autonomous movements in the empirical tests of Chapters 2 and 5.
10. See also section 3.
11. Issues by enterprises are also penalised by the 20 percent tax on coupons, while issues by public entities are exempted and those by semi-public entities bear only a 10 percent tax.
12. A large fraction of the banking system is already controlled by the state, since some of the major banks belong to IRI.
13. Including insurance companies, pension funds, and special credit institutions.
14. See also Section 2. The constraints on banks' portfolios described above, and the ensuing increase in the bond holdings of commercial banks gave rise, together with the increased preference of the public for liquid assets, to what has come to be called 'double intermediation', i.e. the public holds bank deposits, banks hold bonds of special credit institutions, and the latter make long-term loans to firms.
15. See, for instance, Reuber (1964), Dewald and Johnson (1969), Keran (1970), Ranuzzi de Bianchi (1971), Friedlaender (1973), Froyen (1974), Genberg

(1974), Kouri and PorterO1974), Salvemini (1974), Ujiie (1975), Jonson (1976), Sanssapour and Sheen (1976), Bergstrom and Wymer (1976), and Knight and Wymer (1979).

16. All regressions of this chapter are estimated by ordinary least-squared. For reaction functions estimated by two-stage least-square, see Chapter 2.
17. The variable *IIP* has been seasonally adjusted. A note of caution is in order: the sign of the coefficients of *IIP* is quite unstable. It changes depending on whether one seasonally adjusts the series or not, and on what series of domestic assets is used.
18. Results obtained by two-stage least-square do not differ substantially. See Table 2.2 of Chapter 2.
19. This is the only type of systematic neutralisation of reserve flows found in the first two periods.
20. In the figures 3.5, 3.6 and 3.7 the Treasury financing requirement is defined as total Expenditure, minus Revenues and has therefore the opposite sign as in the regressions of Chapter 2, 3 and 5.
21. See Bergstrom and Wymer (1976).
22. See Chapter 2.
23. See Tables 3.1 and 3.2 and Figures 3.5–3.7.

4 Fluctuations in the Exchange Rate of the Lira and Swiss Franc: 1973–8*

INTRODUCTION

In February 1973, the major industrialised countries abandoned the fixed-parity system. Exchange rates were allowed to float, although intervention by monetary authorities was not completely abandoned.

In a floating-rate system in which monetary authorities do intervene, the monetary approach seeks to explain the joint behaviour of two variables: the flow of reserves and the exchange rate. Since cases of total non-intervention in foreign exchange markets are hard to find in practice, problems arise in trying to provide empirical support for the monetary theory of flexible exchange rates. The intervention behaviour of monetary authorities must be explicitly modelled, in the form of an intervention function in which the rate of change of the exchange rate enters as an independent variable. The specification and estimation of such a function is, however, not an easy task and some authors have bypassed the problem by confining the attention of the monetary theory to an *ad hoc* variable which is a weighted average of the rates of change of reserves and of the exchange rate. This weighted average has been called 'exchange market pressure'.[1] The use of such a variable enables the monetary theory to be tested jointly for periods of fixed and flexible exchange rates, and for periods of managed floats. Measures of exchange market pressure, which is itself not an observable quantity, have the disadvantage, however, of being essentially arbitrary, since they depend on the weights chosen to sum exchange-rate and reserve changes.

In this chapter a third approach is considered, which focuses on a particular flexible exchange rate, one that is less subject to the influence of intervention than official rates. This is the exchange rate between the lira and the Swiss franc for bank notes in Zurich for the period February 1973 to December 1978. February 1973 marks the beginning of the floating of the lira; since the Bank of Italy often intervened heavily in the foreign exchange market after that date, the price of Italian bank notes in Zurich tended to fluctuate far more than the rate for cable transfers.[2] Indeed, in some months, the spread between the two rates reached levels of 15 to 20 percent (Figure 4.2). In this chapter the spread is used as the dependent variable in an empirical test of the monetary theory of exchange-rate changes.

The spread was chosen as a dependent variable because it is virtually trendless. In addition, since the market for Italian bank notes is small, relative to that for cable transfers, even large monthly changes in the spread should have very little effect on either the relative inflation rate or relative monetary expansion in the same month. Thus, no reverse causation problem arises in using relative monetary expansion as the main explanatory variable.

The year 1976 saw the most turbulent changes in both exchange rates, and the general fit of the model is somewhat reduced if this year is included in the sample period. Nevertheless, the tests presented here do include the year 1976.

Section 1 presents the monetary approach to flexible exchange rates, but in brief form only, since basic assumptions and implication have already been outlined in Chapter 1. Section 2 contains the empirical tests. Section 3 describes the events leading to the lira crisis in 1976 and Section 4 contains concluding comments.

1. THE MONETARY APPROACH TO FLEXIBLE EXCHANGE RATES

The monetary approach to flexible exchange rates considers the exchange rate as the relative price of two monies. When the money stocks in the two monetary areas are voluntarily held, there is no tendency for the exchange rate to change.

The approach assumes that a stable demand for money, which is a function of a few key variables, exists in both areas, and that arbitrage tends to equate the prices of goods (allowance being made for the different monetary units in the two countries) and the real interest rate on securities. The approach implies that the explanation of the exchange rate is the same whether or not financial markets exist or are integrated with each other. The existence of highly integrated capital markets is, however, assumed to affect the speed of adjustment of the exchange rate to a disturbance.

Some proponents of the theory can be criticised for neglecting equilibrium in financial markets in their formal analyses. Following the classical tradition, developed at a time when financial markets were presumably only rudimentary and could safely be neglected, simple versions of the monetary approach to flexible rates have failed to state explicitly that a stable demand for financial assets in both areas is also assumed and that, because of Walras' Law, financial markets and the market for goods can be neglected in the formal presentation of the model.

Nevertheless, for the limited purposes of this chapter it is sufficient to assume the simple version of the monetary theory of exchange-rate changes, which does not include the demand for financial assets in the formal model.[3]

Equation (1) is a standard text-book demand for cash balances, which is homogeneous of degree one in prices and is a stable function of real income and the expected price level:

$$M_i^D = K_i P_i Y_i^{\alpha} PE_i^{-\beta} = M_i^s \qquad i = I, CH \tag{1}$$

where subscripts $i = I, CH$ refer to Italy and Switzerland, respectively. Y_i is real GNP, a proxy for the volume of transactions in the country (or for wealth); P_i the price level and PE_i the expected price level; and K_i is a constant. Greek letters are elasticities which, for simplicity, are assumed to be equal in the two countries. The equality $M_i^s = M_i^D$ implies equilibrium in the money market.

Equation (2) states that purchasing power parity is assumed to hold in the long run:

$$P_I = \mathrm{ex}\, P_{CH} \tag{2}$$

where 'ex' is the exchange rate, expressed as the number of lire per Swiss franc. This equation reflects the second basic assumption of the monetary approach, namely that arbitrage tends to equate prices across countries. Taking natural logarithms of Equations (1), solving for P_I and P_{CH}, substituting into (2) and solving for 'ex' gives:

(3)

$$\ln ex = \sum_{i=0}^{n1} s_{1i}(\ln M_I - \ln M_{CH})_{t-i} + \sum_{i=1}^{n2} s_{2i}(\ln PE_I - \ln PE_{CH})_{t-i} - \sum_{i=0}^{n3} s_{3i}(\ln Y_I - \ln Y_{CH})_{t-i}$$

where the possibility of time lags has been explicitly taken into account. Equation (3) says that the exchange rate tends to depreciate faster, the greater the rate of relative monetary expansion, the smaller the relative rate of real growth, and the greater the difference in expected price changes.

Using *eo* to indicate the exchange rate between the lira and Swiss franc for cable transfers in Zurich and *e* the market rate for banknotes (also in Zurich), an equation similar to Equation (3) can be written for both exchange rates. Assuming that the rate *e* reacts significantly faster to changes in its explanatory variables than the rate *eo*, ln *eo* can be subtracted from ln *e*; making use of the well-known property of logarithms that $\ln(1+x) \approx x$ for x sufficiently close to zero, one obtains:

(4)

$$\ln\left(\frac{e}{eo}\right) = \ln\left(1 + \frac{e - eo}{eo}\right) \approx \frac{e - eo}{eo} = K + \sum_{i=0}^{n} W_i(\ln M_i - \ln M_{CH})_{t-1} + Z_t$$

Here, the explanatory variables other than money stocks have for simplicity been summarised in the vector Z_t, and a constant term K has been added. Note that it follows from the model that $\sum_{i=1}^{n} W_i = 0$. Testing Equation (4) has an advantage over the test of an equation for ln *e*, such as (3): it represents a test of the importance of relative monetary expansion for the more relevant cable-transfers rate (*eo*), while at the same time the dependent variable is trendless and free from reverse causation.[4]

The hypothesis to be tested is that the sum $\sum_{i=0}^{n} W_i$ is not significantly different from zero, and that the weights W_i first assume positive values and then negative ones, with significant *t*-statistics.

The hypothesis implies that the exchange rate *e* is less sticky, and more sensitive to changes in $(\ln M_I - \ln M_{CH})$, than the rate for cable transfers,

Table 4.1 Spread between the lira and Swiss france exchange rate for banknotes (e) *and cable transfers* (eo) *in Zurich. Monthly data, Feb. 1973–Dec. 1978**

No. of regr.	Constant	$\sum W_i$	I	D_{oil}	D_{RI}	$\ln (TB_I/TB_{CH})$	No. of lags of Almon polyn.	Degree of polyn.	R^2C DW	$\bar{x}$ SER
1	0·005	−0·011†	0·027	0·078	0·059		19	2	0·82	0·048
	(0·21)	(−0·68)	(4·80)	(8·04)	(6·59)				1·17	0·023
2	0·018	−0·021	0·024	0·077	0·052	0·099	19	2	0·84	0·048
	(0·83)	(−1·31)	(4·50)	(8·54)	(5·99)	(3·32)			1·58	0·021
3	0·007	−0·017	0·027	0·078	0·061		19	3	0·82	0·048
	(0·31)	(−0·95)	(4·74)	(8·04)	(6·65)				1·17	0·023

* The Almon polynomials for the variable ($\ln M_I - \ln M_{CH}$) are not constrained.

† The *t*-values of the coefficients of the current and lagged $\ln M_I - \ln M_{CH}$ are: 2·58, 2·55, 2·53, 2·49, 2·39, 2·18, 1·13, −3·49, −3·08, −2·94, −2·87, −2·83, −2·80, −2·79, −2·77, −2·76, −2·75, −2·75, −2·75, −2·74, −2·74.

which is affected more by official intervention. Furthermore, the hypothesis is suggested by the fact that, while the market for e is presumably dominated by capital movements of an illegal nature, the bulk of the market for eo is in commercial transactions which, according to the monetary approach, react with longer lags to relative monetary expansions.[5]

2. EMPIRICAL TESTS

For Italy the money stock chosen was M_2, because in the period in question the (post-tax) rate of return on demand deposits relative to savings deposits has changed, and because studies of the Italian balance of payments have shown that developments in the market for M_2 are more highly correlated with the balance of payments.[6] For Switzerland M_1 was preferred; changes in M_2 might be more sensitive to capital inflows from abroad and hence might be partly endogenous (even under flexible exchange rates).

Table 4.1 contains regressions of $e - eo/eo$ on the current and lagged values of $(\ln M_I - \ln M_{CH})$; on sales of dollars by the Bank of Italy (I) which lead to an increase in the spread; on a dummy for the negative expectations created by the oil crisis; and on a dummy for speculative pressures which followed the resumption of interventions during the lira crisis of 1976.[7] Relative real income was approximated, using indices of industrial production, but was never significantly different from zero. The variable $\ln (TB_I/TB_{CH})$ is the logarithm of the ratio of TB_I to TB_{CH} where TB_I is the ratio of Italian imports of goods to Italian exports and TB_{CH} the same for Switzerland. It reflects expectations about the exchange rate. The experience of the dollar, the mark and the yen in 1977 and 1978 show that the trade balances might be important in affecting the exchange rate directly or via expectations.[8] Regressions 1 and 3 differ only in the degree of the Almon polynomial used for the variable $(\ln M_I - \ln M_{CH})$. The sum of the coefficients of current and lagged $(\ln M_I - \ln M_{CH})$ is not significantly different from zero, as expected, whatever the degree of the Almon polynomial. The time profile of the coefficients of $(\ln M_I - \ln M_{CH})$ in regression 2 and their t-values are shown in Fig. 4.1. The regressions of Table 4.1 show that the effect of relative monetary expansion on the spread $e - eo/eo$ is eliminated, on average, only after about 18 months. Such a long lag is consistent with the finding that under flexible exchange rates, the lag in the response of the Italian current-account balance to Italian excess demand for money is longer than a year.[9] The hypothesis is thus confirmed by the data.

Interventions by the Bank of Italy tend to increase the spread significantly by about 3 percent for every billion dollars sold in the foreign exchange market. The proxy for the expectations about the exchange rate, ln (TB_I/TB_{CH}), tends to increase the exchange-rate spread significantly. The two dummy variables also have the expected sign and are highly significant.

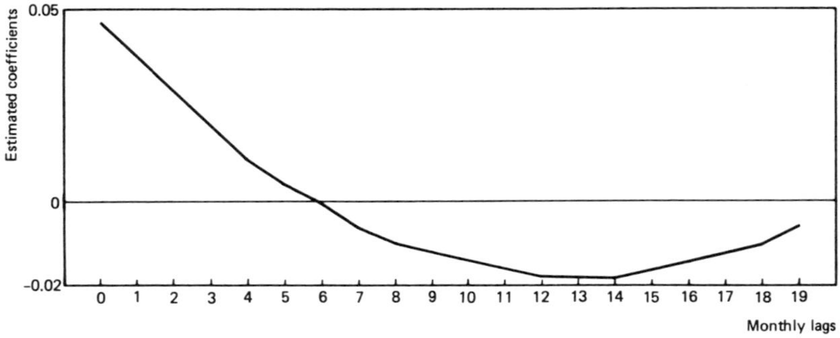

Fig. 4.1 Coefficients of current and lagged ln M_1 − ln M_{CH}. Regression 2, Table 4.1

Fig. 4.2 shows that the fit between actual and expected values of the spread obtained from Regression 2 is generally good.

3. THE LIRA EXCHANGE-RATE CRISIS OF JANUARY–MAY 1976

In 1973, the Italian economy enjoyed a rapid rate of economic growth, fostered by expansionary monetary and fiscal policies. The overall balance of payments, on the definition used in the empirical tests of Chapter 2, was therefore already in a weak (deficit) position when the oil price increase occurred. Moves toward monetary and fiscal restraint were retarded until April 1974 when interest rates were raised sharply. Following the slowdown in world economic growth and, above all, the restrictive economic policy stance taken in April of 1974, real GDP grew only by about 4 percent in 1974 and actually fell by 3½ percent in 1975, as opposed to a growth rate of nominal GDP of about 23 percent for the year 1974 and about 13 percent for the following year.

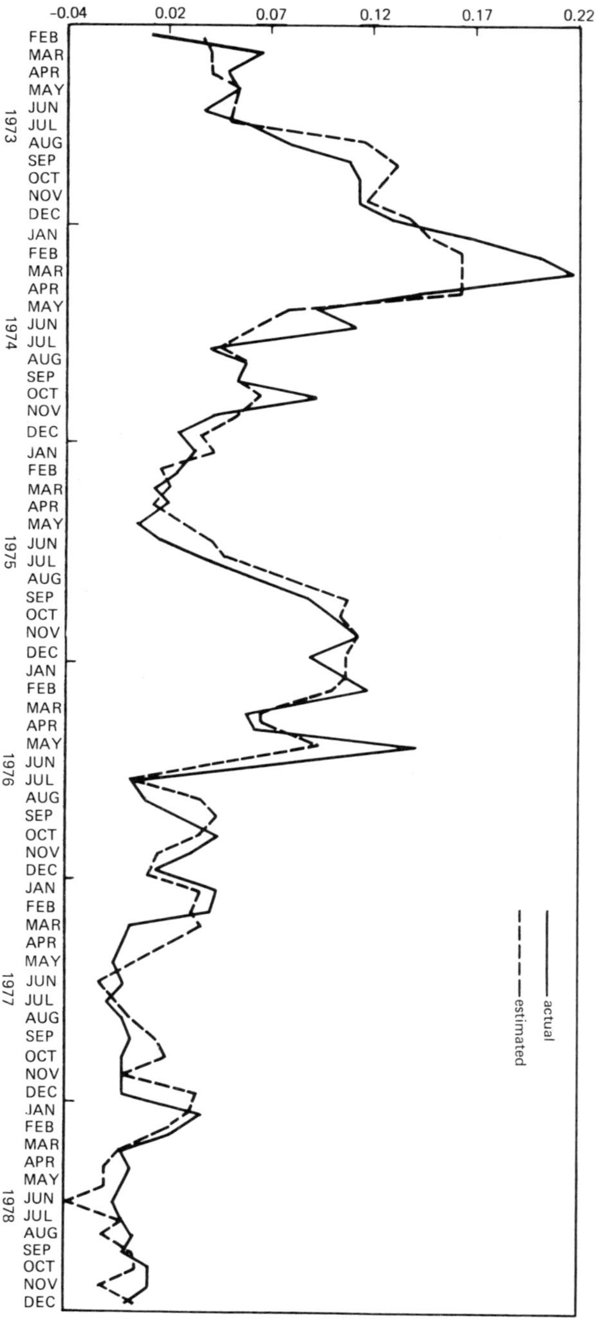

Fig. 4.2 Actual and estimated values of the spread between the lira and Swiss franc exchange rate for banknotes and cable transfers. Regression 2, Table 4.1. Feb. 1973–Dec. 1978

In the second half of 1975, in the face of the unsatisfactory growth in industrial production and employment, political pressures intensified for a reduction in interest rates, and an expansion in demand. The Bank of Italy cautiously allowed the inter-bank deposit rate to fall from 11·7 percent in May to 8·3 percent in December, and the long-term private-bond rate from its peak of 10·9 percent in October to 10·66 percent in December.

However, the reduction in interest rates took place at a time when the Treasury financing requirement was increasing sharply and was putting monetary and financial markets under strain. In the third quarter of 1975 the Treasury financing requirement was almost 4000 billion lire (as opposed to about 2500 billion in the same quarter of 1974), while in the last quarter of 1975 an unexpected increase of about 2000 billion lire brought the total to almost 5500 billion (as opposed to a little over 2000 billion in the last quarter of 1974). The Bank of Italy was therefore compelled to acquire Treasury bonds and bills in much larger amounts than expected. This increase in the monetary base was not consistent with the continued stability in the exchange rate which had been pursued throughout the year, despite the worsening of the current account. The latter moved from a surplus of more than 600 billion lire in the first half of 1975 to a deficit of more than 700 billion in the third quarter and more than 1000 billion in the fourth. The fall in international reserves intensified sharply toward the end of the year. A huge additional loss of international reserves took place in the first 20 days of 1976, leaving the Bank of Italy with very little reserves. As a result, the official quotation of the lira and its support by the Bank of Italy was abandoned on January 21st. The price of Italian bank notes in Zurich, which was already 8 percent lower than the official rate in December 1975, fell by 6 percent in January (compared to 4 percent for the official rate), by 12 percent in February (11 percent), by 2 percent in March (7 percent), and by a further 9 percent in April (8 percent). Toward the end of April the fall of the exchange rate accelerated, possibily for political reasons.[10]

On May 6th, a non-interest-bearing deposit was introduced on all future purchases of foreign exchange. The deposit was equal to 50 percent of the amount of foreign exchange required, and was to be held for 90 days at the Bank of Italy.

The implications of the sharp increase in the Treasury financing requirement for Italian monetary expansion are summarised in Table 4.2. The rates of change of the Swiss money supply (M_1) are also reported. It will be recalled from the previous section that the Italian and

Swiss money stocks were regarded as the main determinants of the spread between the price of Italian bank notes in Zurich and the official rate.

Table 4.2 Rates of increase of Italian M_2 *and Swiss* M_1. *Annualised rates*

	$\dot{M}_I$	$\dot{M}_{CH}$	$\dot{M}_I - \dot{M}_{CH}$
1975–10	11·04	18·84	– 7·80
11	11·04	40·27	– 29·23
12	104·64	55·20	49·44
1976–1	3·48	– 28·44	31·92
2	8·52	– 30·24	38·76
3	22·97	30·48	– 7·51
4	7·60	11·40	– 3·80
5	11·04	– 8·64	19·68
6	7·39	36·60	– 29·21
7	8·22	– 25·68	33·90

Source: Banca d'Italia, *Bollettino* and Schweizerische Nationalbank, *Monatsbericht*.

The third column of Table 4.2 shows the difference between the rates of change of the two money stocks. The rise in the difference in December 1975 and January – February 1976 is huge and goes a long way towards explaining the pressure on the lira.

4. CONCLUSIONS

The chapter has presented an empirical analysis of fluctuations in the spread between the exchange rates for the lira and Swiss franc in the market for bank notes and for cable transfers in Zurich. This spread has the advantage of being trendless and free from reverse causation with relative monetary expansion, because of the small size of the market for bank notes. The hypothesis under test is that the price of Italian bank notes in Zurich, being less influenced by official intervention and involving mainly illegal capital outflows, reacts much faster to relative monetary expansion than the exchange rate for cable transfers, which ultimately, however, also has to adjust to relative monetary disturbances.

Formally, the hypothesis reduces to testing whether the sum of current and lagged values of (ln $M_I - M_{CH}$) is insignificantly different from zero. The empirical tests, besides showing a good fit, confirm the hypothesis. The tests presented, however, have a number of shortcomings: the equation tested is a reduced-form equation and the impact of real magnitudes and demand-management policies other than monetary policy have been neglected. Furthermore, the number of dummy variables used is relatively large, although they have been included only when the actual circumstances of the period justified this.

APPENDIX 4.1 SYMBOLS AND SOURCES OF DATA USED

e = exchange rate between lira and Swiss franc (banknotes) expressed as number of lire per Swiss franc, average of daily figures. Source: Schweizerische Nationalbank, *Monatsbericht*, various issues.

eo = exchange rate between lira and Swiss franc (cable transfers), number of lire per Swiss franc, average of daily figures. Source: Schweizerische Nationalbank, *Monatsbericht*, various issues.

I = gross sales of dollars in the foreign exchange market by the Bank of Italy (billions of dollars). Source: Unpublished series, Bank of Italy.

ln = natural logarithm

M_{CH} = Swiss M_1. Source: Schweizerische Nationalbank, *Monatsbericht*, various issues.

M_I = Italian M_2, defined as overall deposits of commercial banks plus currency in circulation. Source: Banca d'Italia, *Bollettino*.

TB_I = ratio of Italian imports of goods to Italian exports, seasonally adjusted. Source: International Monetary Fund, *International Financial Statistics*, lines 71 and 70.

TB_{CH} = ratio of Swiss imports of goods to Swiss exports, seasonally adjusted. Source: International Monetary Fund, *International Financial Statistics*, lines 71 and 70.

D_{oil} = dummy variable for negative expectations about the future of the lira, because of the outbreak of the oil crisis. Assumes the value of +1 in the period August 1973 to March 1974, and zero otherwise.

D_{RI} = dummy used for the resumption of interventions in the foreign exchange market during the exchange crisis of the first half of 1976. Assumes the value of +1 in April, May, June and July of 1976, and zero otherwise.

NOTES TO CHAPTER 4

* A shortened version of this chapter has been published in the *European Economic Review*, 12 (Feb. 1979). The empirical estimates contained in the above article cover the period Feb. 1973-Dec. 1976, while here they cover the period up to Dec. 1978.

1. The concept of exchange market pressure was introduced by Girton and Roper (1977).
2. I am grateful to Giovanni De Cindio for first drawing my attention to this exchange rate and its higher variability relative to the official rate.
3. For models which also formally include financial asset markets, see Dornbusch (1976) and Basevi and De Grauwe (1977); for the monetary theory of the balance of payments, see Dornbusch (1975) ajd Rodriguez (1976).
4. Test of Equation (3) for the rate *e* are not shown in this chapter; see Tullio (1978).
5. See Swoboda (1973), and Chapter 5.
6. Chapter 2, Section 2.
7. Monetary policy became very restrictive and interest rates were sharply increased only in April 1974, after a long period of pegging. Since most of the large industrialised countries had already started to tighten monetary policy in the middle of 1973, the outbreak of the oil crisis generated expectations of a sharp depreciation of the lira. D_{oil} therefore assumes the value of +1 from Aug. 1973 to Mar. 1974. The very restrictive monetary policy started in Apr. 1974, had by the end of the same year led to a marked improvement in the current account and this produced expectations of a smaller depreciation or a higher appreciation of the lira, which may be reflected in the significant coefficient of $\ln(TB_I/TB_{CH})$. After 1973, the period of strongest depreciation of the lira started in Feb. 1976, following a sharp acceleration of monetary expansion in Italy at the end of 1975. At the end of January the official foreign exchange market was closed and the official rate could fluctuate almost freely. It followed that, in March particularly, the rate *eo* was in a position to depreciate more quickly than predicted by the model. Finally, at the beginning of May the depreciation of both exchange rates was ended by the introduction of a deposit scheme on all imports. The dummy D_{RI} assumes a value of +1 in April, May, June and July of 1976 and zero otherwise, and it reflects the negative effects on the exchange rate for banknotes of the resumption of official interventions in the foreign exchange market. See, also, Appendix 4.1 which contains symbols and sources of data used.
8. The variable $(\ln P_I - \ln P_{CH})_{t-1}$ which is supposed to measure not only the relative expected price level (see equation (1)) but also the expected depreciation of the lira, loses its significance when the sample period is extended from the end of 1976 to the end of 1978. Compare Table 4.2 with the

results obtained in Tullio (1979b). Relative interest-rate changes were also tried as a proxy for relative inflationary expectations but without success. Italian rates do not show sufficient variability from month to month, because they have been pegged throughout most of the period.

9. See Chapter 5.
10. In April it was decided to hold general elections in June.

5 Speed of Adjustment of the Capital and the Current Accounts to Money Market Disturbances: Some Empirical Findings

INTRODUCTION

Empirical work on the monetary approach to the balance of payments has tended to concentrate up to now on the reaction of the overall balance of payments, or of the exchange rate, to money market disturbances without investigating separately the reaction pattern of the current and the capital accounts.[1] The empirical work presented in Chapter 2 does not depart from this tradition.

The overall balance of payments is generally regressed either on the main arguments of the demand and supply functions for money, the parameters being estimated by the two-stage least-square method in order to avoid the reverse causation problem between changes in the domestic assets of the central bank and the balance of payments; or directly on a constructed measure of excess demand for money.[2]

Proponents of the monetary approach maintain that the non-existence of capital movements does not affect the nature of the mechanism of adjustment of the balance of payments, but that it affects its speed of adjustment, as the capital account reacts faster (Swoboda, 1973). Indeed, classical balance-of-payments theory, of which the modern literature on the monetary approach is a re-formulation, has been to a large extent developed at a time when capital movements were either non-existent or empirically unimportant, and were in any case neglected in theoretical formulations. The balance of payments which, owing to the irrelevance of capital movements, was considered identical to the current account (or the trade balance) was explained by disequilibria between the 'natural' quantity of money that the economic system could absorb[3] and the quantity that was supplied.

In this chapter the reaction pattern of the Italian current and capital accounts to money market disturbances will be investigated separately. A demand function for M_1 will be estimated on quarterly data[4] and a measure of ex-ante flow excess demand for money will be constructed on which both the capital and the current account will be regressed along with other explanatory variables like the government budget deficit. This will allow us to see to what extent the excess demand for money is able to explain both items of the balance of payments and to what extent the reaction pattern of the two items differs.

In order to place the discussion in a broader context Section 1 will be devoted to a brief comparison between the monetary approach and the so-called Cambridge view, which places primary emphasis on the government budget deficit in the explanation of the current account. This comparison seems particularly appropriate not only because the Cambridge view has attracted some attention in recent years, but above all because, as we have seen in Chapters 2 and 3, the Treasury financing requirement has been the primary force behind the increase in domestic assets of the Bank of Italy at least roughly speaking from 1966 to 1976.

In Section 2 the model is set out. Empirical tests of the Italian current and capital accounts on the constructed measures of excess demand for money are presented for the fixed exchange rate period in Section 3. In Section 4 some interesting extensions to the flexible exchange rate period are presented.

1. EXPLANATION OF THE CURRENT ACCOUNT: THE MONETARY APPROACH VERSUS THE CAMBRIDGE VIEW

The Cambridge view, developed by a group of economists at the University of Cambridge,[5] assumes that there is a demand for the net acquisition of financial assets by the private sector, which is a stable function of disposable income and its first difference.[6] Interest rates do not appear in the function. From the existence of such a stable relationship and the neglect of the interest rate in the function, coupled with the existence of unemployed resources, the Cambridge view infers that an increase in the budget deficit generates an equal increase in the current-account deficit (or a reduction in the surplus), *independently of how the deficit is financed.* Thus, while both the monetary approach and the Cambridge view recognise the role of stocks, the latter approach centres upon a demand for overall net financial assets, without distinguishing within its various components, while at the same time playing down the role of interest rates. An important consequence of this neglect of interest rates and the composition of financial assets, is that the Cambridge view rules out the possibility of a crowding-out of private expenditure by public expenditure in the case of an increase in the public-sector deficit being financed by selling bonds to the public (i.e. by increasing the interest rate), instead of by printing money. The implication of the Cambridge view, that a rise in interest rates will not in itself induce the public to increase its holdings of government bonds nor have any effect on private expenditure, has, in general, led to a rejection of the approach in Italy. This was particularly the case after 1976, when the change in interest-rate policy outlined in Chapter 4 led to a larger proportion of the increasing public-sector deficit being financed by sales of bonds to the public, and both the capital and the current accounts of the balance of payments swung into an unprecedented surplus.

In order to clarify further the assumptions and implications of the approaches we shall sketch below how we think that in a general equilibrium framework an increase in the public-sector deficit is likely to affect the current account in the two extreme cases in which there are unused resources and in which income is already at or close to being fully employed.

We shall assume throughout that exchange rates are pegged.

A. If unused resources exist in the economy and prices are fixed, an increase in the public-sector deficit is likely to lead, with a relatively short lag, to an increase in output, in disposable income and in imports. If all of the increased budget deficit is financed by money creation, the increase in the demand for money due to a higher level of transactions will fall short of the increase in the supply, and interest rates will tend to fall. The capital account will thus be affected negatively, but the current account will also worsen by more than the increase in the budget deficit if private expenditure is affected by the fall in the interest rate. If, instead, the increased budget deficit is financed by sales of bonds to the public, the increased demand for bonds due to an increase in disposable income will fall short of the increased supply, and the interest rate will tend to rise. Again, unless private expenditure is insensitive to changes in the interest rate, the current-account deficit will not increase by the same amount as the budget deficit, but by less.

However, the departure from the simple Cambridge conclusion that the increase in the budget deficit leads to a worsening of the current account by the same amount, is not likely to be large, especially if the interest elasticity of private expenditure is low. In general, therefore, when a large pool of unused resources exists, the Cambridge view is a reasonable enough simplification of reality, and its neglect of the way in which the Government deficit is financed is not too misleading. This conclusion, however, changes dramatically when the economy is at, or close to, full-employment conditions and fiscal policy cannot stimulate the level of economic activity.

We now move on, therefore, to discuss the next case.

B. If the economy is at, or near, full employment and inflationary expectations are not fixed, fiscal policy is not in a position to increase output to any great extent, and the demand for money and bonds is not affected positively, as in the previous case. Hence, the excess supply of money, if the budget deficit is financed by money creation, or the excess supply of bonds, if the deficit is financed only by sales of bonds, is larger than in the previous case, particularly if expansionary fiscal policy leads to an upward revision of inflationary expectations, which in turn affects negatively the propensity to hold money and bonds, other things being equal. When the budget deficit is entirely financed by money creation, national expenditure will exceed national output and imports will exceed exports – at least, as long as there are foreign exchange reserves to sustain the foreign imbalance. If, however, the budget deficit is entirely financed by sales of bonds, the real interest rate has to go up, and for a given interest elasticity of domestic expenditures, the level of private expenditure and imports will be affected more negatively than in the case of bond financing when unused resources exist, because of the larger increase in interest rates. In the limiting case of a total crowding-out of private expenditure, the current account will not be affected by the increase in the budget deficit.

The case in which income is at, or almost at, the full-employment level, and inflationary expectations are not sticky, probably comes closer to representing Italy's situation in the 1960s and 1970s.[8] Thus, it appears likely that the Cambridge view that the worsening of the current account is equal to the increase in the budget deficit applies only in the case of money financing of the budget deficit, and even in that case only in a short-term view, since capital movements are likely to speed up considerably the loss in reserves.

In Section 2 a very simple model will be presented which neglects the dynamics of adjustment of the current account to fiscal disturbances, but which serves the purpose of showing that the public-sector borrowing requirement had, in the case of Italy, no independent effect on the current account and that the way it was financed was therefore very important.

2. THE MODEL

We assume that the demand function for real money narrowly defined (m) is given by (1):

$$(1) \qquad m^* = \frac{M}{p} = Ay^{\alpha y} f^{\alpha f}$$

where an asterisk refers to desired quantities, p is the consumer price index, A is a constant, y is real GNP, f is the opportunity cost of holding money, and the α's are elasticities. We assume further that actual real balances adjust to the desired quantity according to (2):

$$(2) \qquad \ln m - \ln m_{-1} = \lambda(\ln m^* - \ln m_{-1})$$

where λ is the adjustment parameter of actual to desired balances. By substituting (1) and (2) one obtains an equation for m which can be tested, because all variables are observable:

$$(3) \qquad \ln m = a + b \ln y + c \ln f + d \ln m_{-1}$$

Equation (3) has been tested for money narrowly defined (m_1) on quarterly data from 1964–I to 1971–IV, during which period Italy maintained fixed exchange rates with the rest of the world, and from 1972 to 1978, a time when exchange rates were more flexible. The division into two periods differs from that adopted in Chapters 2 and 3, mainly because of the additional concern here with capital movements; in 1972 restrictions on capital outflows became considerably more severe than previously.

Returning to Equation (3), it is well known that estimates of the elasticities αy, αf and of λ can be obtained from the estimates of the coefficients of (3) according to (4):

$$(4) \qquad \alpha y = \frac{b}{1-d}; \qquad \alpha f = \frac{c}{1-d}; \qquad \lambda = 1 - d$$

The values obtained are all in a plausible range: $\alpha y = 1{\cdot}56$ for the first period and 0·80 for the second.[9]

The excess demand for money was then defined as follows (*ex ante* flow excess demand for money):

$$EDM = M_{t-1}\left(\dot{m}_t^* - \frac{(\dot{DA})_t}{P}\right) \tag{5}$$

where a dot above the variable indicates a percentage change, DA represents the domestic assets of the Bank of Italy, and $\dot{m}_t^*$ is obtained from (1) by using the estimated elasticities. The fact that the measure of the excess demand for money includes DA reflects the belief that for a small country linked to the rest of the world by fixed or pegged exchange rates, the only exogenous monetary aggregate is DA and that movements in this aggregate best represent the pressure on the money market coming from the supply side.[10]

In the next section the Italian capital and current account will be regressed on current and lagged values of *ex-ante* flow excess demand for money according to:

$$CAP_t = \beta_0 + \sum_{i=0}^{n} j_i\, EDM_{t-i} + \delta L_t + u_t \tag{6}$$

$$CUR_t = \beta'_0 + \sum_{i=1}^{m} j'_i\, EDM_{t-i} + \delta' L'_t + u'_t \tag{7}$$

where CAP_t is the capital account and CUR_t is the current account in quarter t, δ is a vector of parameters and L a vector of variables to be specified in the next section, and u is the error term with the usual properties.

In equation (7) the vector L'_t includes the Treasury financing requirement (*TFR*). Its inclusion aims at testing whether the government deficit exerted an effect on the current account independently of the way it was financed. The three propositions of the monetary approach that one wishes to test are:

a) that the excess demand for money (*EDM*) explains reasonably well both the current and the capital accounts;

b) that $m > n$ (see Swoboda, 1973) i.e. that the capital account adjusts faster than the current account; and

c) that, contrary to the Cambridge view, the Treasury financing requirement (*TFR*) does not affect the current account.

*Table 5.1 Italian capital movements on excess demand for money. Quarterly data, 1964–71**

No. of regr.	CUR	EDM	EDM_{-1}	EDM_{-2}	EDM_{-3}	EDM_{-4}	R^2	R^2C	DW	SER $\bar{x}$
1	−0·78 (−9·21)	0·038 (2·74)	0·055 (2·70)	0·052 (2·53)	0·030 (1·66)	−0·013 (−0·58)	0·69	0·67	1·48	239·5 339·2

* Data are not seasonally adjusted; for the variable *EDM* the Almon polynomial lag-estimation technique has been used (second degree polymonial, constrained to zero on the right and on the left).

It should be pointed out that the excess demand for money is expressed in an arbitrary unit of measure and therefore no particular meaning should be attached to the size of its coefficients. Its interest lies in its explanatory power, in the number of its significant lags, in the comparison of the size of its coefficients in the regressions explaining the capital and the current account, and in the possibility of significant changes in its lag structure after 1972.

3. REACTION PATTERN OF THE ITALIAN CAPITAL AND CURRENT ACCOUNTS TO MONETARY DISTURBANCES UNDER FIXED EXCHANGE RATES

We shall present first the regressions relating to the capital account. Table 5.1 contains ordinary least-square estimates of Equation (6), based on quarterly data from 1964 to 1971. During this period Italy maintained perfectly fixed exchange rates with the rest of the world, and in addition the period can be considered uniform from the point of view of existing restrictions on capital movements.[11]

The number of lags of the excess demand for money was chosen according to a non-negativity constraint (with the first negative lag shown in the regression) and the estimation was performed using the Almon polynomial lag-estimation technique. The constant term was never significantly different from zero. Another variable added along with the excess demand for money is that for current account.[12]

Regression 1 is extremely satisfactory in terms of overall explanatory power and significance of the variable one is mainly interested in here (*EDM*); it indicates that money market disturbances exerted all their effects on the Italian capital account in the period under study within three to four quarters.

The empirical tests of Equation (7) for the fixed exchange-rate period are presented in Table 5.2. The parameters of *EDM* have been estimated by using the Almon polynomial lag-estimation technique. The number of lags has been chosen according to the non-negativity criterion. A number of variables have been added to the independent variables of Equation (7):

P_x/P_{xw} is the ratio of Italian export prices to the export prices of Italy's main competitors. In general, it is not significant. Neither is the Treasury financing requirement, which, in addition, has the wrong sign. It seems, therefore, that an increase in the Treasury financing requirement, not financed by money creation, did not exert any impact on the current

*Table 5.2 Italian current account balance, seasonally adjusted, on excess demand for money**

No. of regr.	Sample period	Lags	*EDM*	*TFR*	P_x/P_{xw}	Constant	DW ρ‡	SER $\bar{x}$	R^2	R^2C
2†	1964–I	t	0·035 (2·14)		−1270·4 (−0·68)	−739·3 (−0·34)	1·84	103·2	0·69	0·61
	to	$t-1$	0·045 (3·09)		2458·0 (1·26)		0·46	426·8		
	1971–IV	$t-2$	0·050 (3·28)							
		$t-3$	0·052 (3·26)							
		$t-4$	0·050 (3·26)							
		$t-5$	0·043 (3·12)							
		$t-6$	0·033 (2·21)							
		$t-7$	0·019 (0·89)							
3	1962–II	$t-$	0·058 (2·74)	−0·077 (−0·79)	62·8 (0·04)	901·6 (0·39)	1·60	117·9	0·83	0·75
	to	$t-1$	0·041 (1·83)	−0·062 (−0·61)	−470·8 (−0·28)		0·80	372·1		
	1971–IV	$t-2$	0·024 (1·01)							
		$t-3$	0·085 (3·19)							
		$t-4$	0·070 (2·36)							
		$t-5$	0·037 (1·41)							

* *EDM*, *TFR* and the dependent variable are seasonally adjusted.

† For the variable *EDM*, the Almon polynomial lag-estimation technique has been used (polynomial of second order, no constraints).

‡ ρ is the coefficient of autocorrelation, where the correction for autocorrelation has been performed by using the Cochrane–Orcutt technique.

account, contrary to the prediction of the Cambridge view. The near-full-employment conditions which prevailed in Italy during the period 1964–71 seem to have rendered the Cambridge view irrelevant. As we concluded in Section 1, under near-full-employment conditions it is the way the budget deficit is financed that matters. This conclusion is reinforced by the fact that regressions of the current account on the Treasury financing requirement only[13] have an extremely low explanatory power and the independent variable is still insignificant. As we shall see in the Section 4 for the flexible exchange-rate period, too, the empirical tests strongly support the monetary approach view and lead us to reject the Cambridge view.

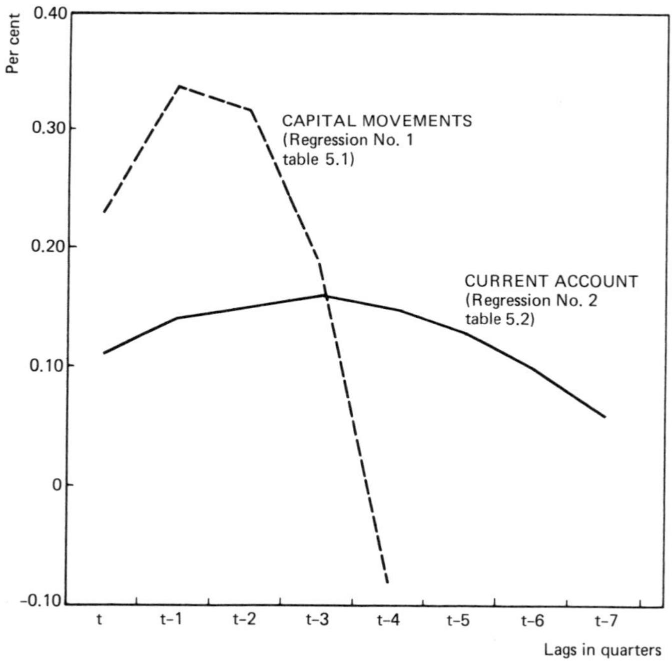

Fig. 5.1 Time profile of the effects of monetary disequilibrium on the capital and current accounts under fixed exchange rates (as percentage of total effect)

The coefficients of *EDM* in Regression 3 are depicted in Figure 5.1. Together with the coefficients of *EDM* taken from Regression 1, Figure 5.1 shows that, while money market disturbances (which include both domestic real and monetary disturbances) influence the capital account within three to four quarters, the effect on the current account seems to work itself out within seven to eight quarters.

By way of conclusion one can therefore say that:

a) Regressions 1 to 3 show that our measure of excess demand for money explains satisfactorily both the current and the capital accounts of the balance of payments, and that therefore the theory underlying the explanation of both items seems to be the same;

b) the speed of adjustment of the capital account has been substantially faster than the speed of adjustment of the current account;

c) the data seem to contradict the Cambridge view.

Figure 5.2 shows the actual and expected values obtained from Regression 3 of Table 2

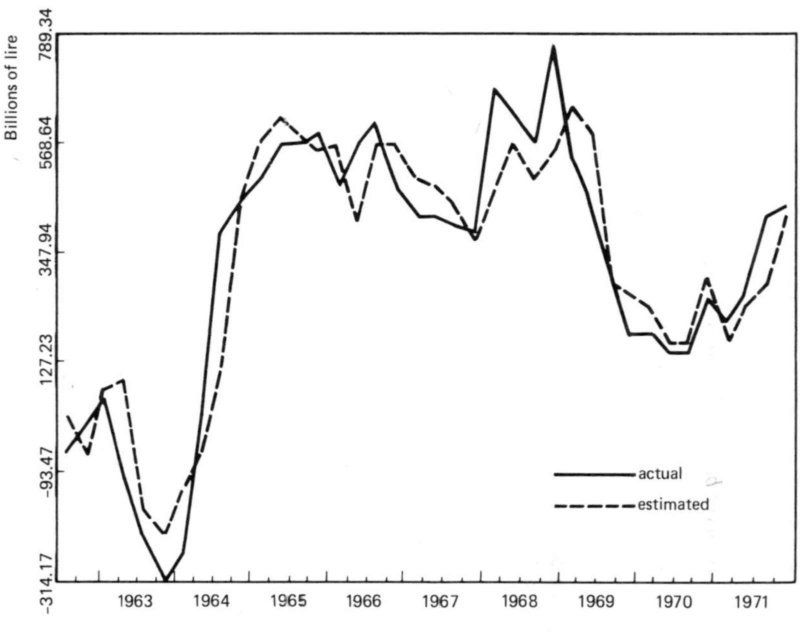

Fig. 5.2 Italian current account balance, seasonally adjusted, billions of lire: 1962–III to 1971–IV. Estimated values obtained from regression 3, Table 5.2

4. AN EXTENSION TO THE FLEXIBLE EXCHANGE-RATE PERIOD, AND CONCLUSIONS

From the end of 1971 the exchange rate of the lira was frequently adjusted until, in February 1973, a central parity was abandoned

*Table 5.3 Italian current account balance, seasonally adjusted, on excess demand for money. Quarterly data, 1972–8**

No. of regr.	Lags	*EDM*	*TFR*	$\dot{e}$†	Constant	DW ρ	SER $\bar{x}$	R^2	R^2C
4‡	t	0·057 (3·40)		5023·9 (2·19)	320·83 (1·61)	1·83	337·5	0·87	0·83
	$t-1$	0·053 (4·47)		−847·5 (−0·37)		0·58	662·55		
	$t-2$	0·048 (4·16)		−2034·9 (−0·88)					
	$t-3$	0·042 (3·52)							
	$t-4$	0·036 (3·15)							
	$t-5$	0·029 (2·73)							
	$t-6$	0·022 (1·61)							
	$t-7$	0·014 (0·62)							
5	t	0·058 (2·95)	−0·006 (−0·11)	4769·4 (2·00)	−216·7 (−0·47)	1·80	330·7	0·91	0·84
	$t-1$	0·077 (3·11)	0·089 (1·67)	−2424·5 (−1·03)		0·70	662·55		
	$t-2$	0·064 (2·23)		−4288·2 (−1·55)					
	$t-3$	0·060 (0·19)							
	$t-4$	0·038 (1·29)							

* *EDM*, *TFR* and dependent variable are seasonally adjusted.

† Effective exchange rate changes; source: International Monetary Fund, *International Financial Statistics*. An exchange rate depreciation implies $\dot{e} < 0$, hence a positive sign of the coefficient implies a worsening of the current account.

‡ For the excess demand for money the Almon polynomial lag-estimation technique has been used (polynomial of second order and no constraint).

altogether, although interventions by the Bank of Italy in the foreign exchange market continued at times on a heavy scale. Under these conditions it does not make much sense to extend the period of estimation of the capital account (Equation (6)) beyond 1971, although it might be of interest to extend the estimation of the current account (Equation (7)) beyond 1971. A demand for real-money balances, narrowly defined, has therefore been estimated with quarterly data from 1972 to 1978.[14] The measure of excess demand for money has then been constructed using the elasticities obtained.

The ordinary least-square estimates of Equation (7) for the period 1972–I to 1978–IV are shown in Table 5.3. The main explanatory variable, *EDM*, has been lagged by using the Almon polynomial lag-estimation technique.

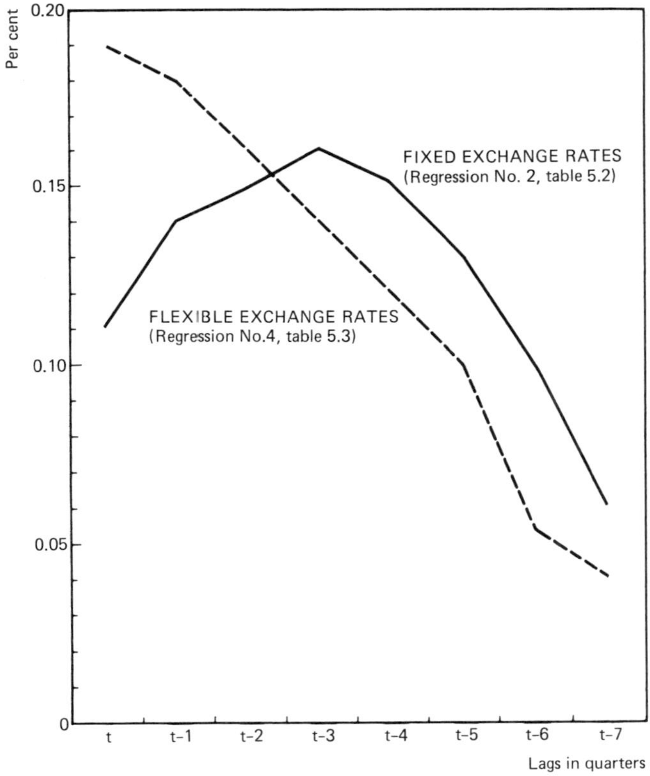

Fig. 5.3 Time profile of the effects of monetary disequilibrium on the current account under fixed and flexible exchange rates (as percentage of total effect)

Again the Treasury financing requirement is never significant (Regression 5), while a depreciation of the effective exchange rate ($\dot{e}$) has a significant negative impact on the current account in the first quarter. By comparing the coefficients of *EDM* of regression 2 of Table 5.2 with those of Regression 4 of Table 5.3 one obtains Figure 5.3. Figure 5.3 shows that the speed of adjustment of the current account to money market disturbances has increased in the flexible exchange-rate period. This can be explained as follows:

a) Italian monetary authorities have sharply increased the côntrol on all kinds of capital movements in the more recent period, and the series of the current account used in Table 5.3 hides a large portion of capital movements (although it has been previously corrected by using existing estimates of capital movements hidden in the items 'tourism' and 'remittances from labour income' of the current account (see Appendix 5.1));

b) the increased instability of monetary and real variables in the period from 1972 to 1978 might have increased the reaction pattern of the current account to money market disturbances.

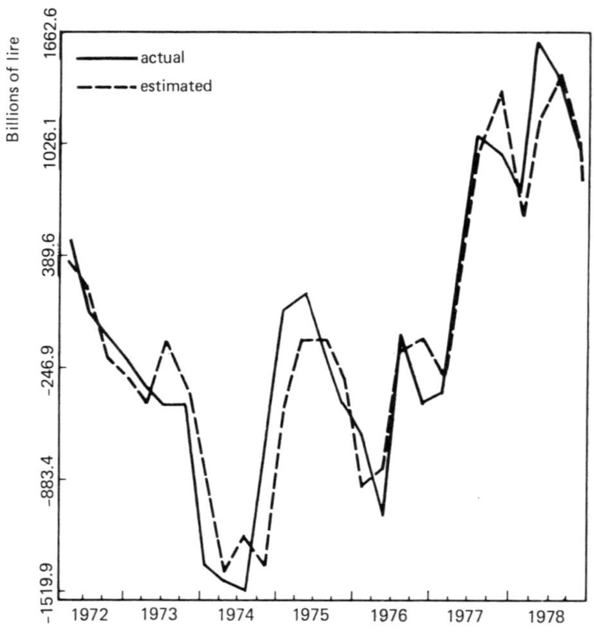

Fig. 5.4 Italian current account balance, seasonally adjusted, billions of lire: 1972–II to 1978–IV. Estimated values obtained from regression 4, Table 5.3

Figure 5.4 shows the actual and estimated values obtained from Regression 4 of Table 5.3.

This chapter has tried to analyse the speed of adjustment of the current and capital accounts to money market disturbances by constructing an arbitrary measure of excess demand for real-money balances. It has been shown that the proposition of classical balance-of-payments theory (and of the monetary approach) that developments in the money market are central to the outcome of the current account and not merely of the capital account seems to be true, at least in the case of Italy. It has also been shown that the Cambridge view does not have much explanatory power in the case of Italy, under both fixed and flexible exchange rates.

Furthermore, it has been shown that under fixed exchange rates the speed of adjustment of the capital account is considerably higher than the speed of adjustment of the current account (see Swoboda, 1973), as one would expect in theory.

Finally, in Section 5.4 we have seen that the speed of adjustment of the Italian current account increased after 1972, both because of extensive controls on capital movements and probably also because of increased instability in that period.

APPENDIX 1: LIST OF SYMBOLS AND SOURCES OF DATA USED

CAP = Italian capital account. The series has been obtained as follows: The official definition of the overall balance of payments (Source: Bank of Italy, *Bollettino*) has been corrected for compensating loans obtained for balance-of-payments purposes by the Italian monetary authorities (from 1969) and for changes in the net foreign position of the Italian commercial banking system. (The latter net position, although largely autonomous, is included below the line among compensating movements.) The official series of the current account (Source: Bank of Italy, *Bollettino*) has been subtracted from the series of the overall balance of payments obtained above. Finally, the series of the overall capital account thus obtained has been corrected by incorporating into it the existing estimates of capital outflows hidden in the items 'tourism' and 'remittances from labour income' of the current account for the years 1970,

1971, and 1972. The estimates were obtained from Carlo Chiesa (1975). For the years prior to 1970 the capital outflows hidden in the above items were irrelevant, and from the year 1973 the correction has been incorporated into the official statistics.

CUR = Italian current account, appropriately corrected (see above). The official series has been taken from the Bank of Italy's *Bollettino* (*bilancia economica*, i.e. statistics obtained from customs declarations).

d = first difference of a variable.

DA = domestic assets of the Bank of Italy (Source: International Monetary Fund, *International Financial Statistics*, Line 12a plus line 12e).

e = percentage change of the effective exchange rate of the lira (Source: International Monetary Fund, *International Financial Statistics*).

EDM = *ex ante* flow excess demand for money $= M\left[\dot{m}^* - \left(\frac{\dot{DA}}{P}\right)\right]$

ln = natural logarithm

P = consumer price index (Source: International Monetary Fund, *International Financial Statistics*, line 64).

P_x = Italian unit values of exports (Source: International Monetary Fund, *International Financial Statistics*).

P_{xw} = unit values of exports of industrialised countries, excluding Italy (Source: International Monetary Fund).

r = Italian long-term interest rate on Treasury bonds (Source: Bank of Italy, *Bollettino*).

rr $= \left(\frac{r_{d/d} - r_{s/d}}{100} + 1\right)$, where $r_{d/d}$ is the interest rate on demand deposits and $r_{s/d}$ the interest on savings deposits (Source: Bank of Italy, *Bollettino*).

TFR = Treasury financing requirement (Source: Bank of Italy, *Supplemento al Bollettino*).

y = Italian quarterly GNP (Source: *Istituto Nazionale per lo Studio della Congiuntura*, Rome).

NOTES TO CHAPTER 5

1. One exception is represented by Kouri and Porter (1974). See also Tullio (1977).

2. See, for example, the empirical tests presented in Chapter 2.
3. See chapter 1.
4. The demand functions for money used in Chapter 2, Section 2 were estimated on annual data and the time period was different.
5. See Nield (1973), Godley and Cripps (1974, 1976).
6. Also that the net increase in consumer hire-purchase debt; bank advances to the personal sector and the increase in the value of stocks are assumed to affect the net acquisition of financial assets negatively and hence private expenditure positively. Assuming such a stable demand for net financial assets is equivalent to assuming that there exists a stable relationship between private expenditure and private disposable income, and this is recognised by the Cambridge view.
8. Despite the increase in unemployment in the 1970s a large fraction of it is probably of a structural nature.
9. The ordinary least-square estimation of Equation 3 yields:

$$\ln m = -1{\cdot}7 + 0{\cdot}81 \ln m_{-1} + 0{\cdot}29 \ln y + 10{\cdot}46 \ln rr$$

$$(-1.18) \quad (10.46) \qquad (1.56) \qquad (1.80)$$

$$R^2C = 0{\cdot}99 \qquad \text{D.W.} = 2{\cdot}19 \qquad \text{SER} = 0{\cdot}0266$$

Numbers in parenthesis are t-statistics and the period of estimation is from 1964–I to 1971–IV; rr is the opportunity cost of holding demand deposits with respect to savings deposits. The stock of money has not been seasonally adjusted.

10. It should be pointed out that in the case of Italy the results of Chapters 2 and 3 show that there is no systematic reaction of changes in DA to the overall balance of payments.
11. See Biagioli (1975).
12. See Kouri and Porter (1974) for a justification of the inclusion of the current account.
13. The regressions are not shown here.
14. The estimated real demand for money function is:

$$\ln m = -0{\cdot}40 + 0{\cdot}62 \ln m_{-1} + 0{\cdot}30 \ln y - 0{\cdot}11 \ln r$$

$$(-0{\cdot}35) \quad (5{\cdot}48) \qquad (2{\cdot}32) \quad (-3.37)$$

$$R^2C^2 = 0{\cdot}74 \qquad \text{DW} = 1{\cdot}92 \qquad \text{x} = 0{\cdot}92$$

where r is the long-term interest rate on Treasury bonds and x is the autocorrelation coefficient (autocorrelation corrected by Cochrane-Orcutt technique). The period of estimation is from 1971–IV to 1978–IV. The time series have been seasonally adjusted and stock variables integrated.

Bibliography

Aghevli, Bijan B., and Khan, Moshin S., 'The Monetary Approach to Balance of Payments Determination: An Empirical Test', Washington, D.C., Asian Department, International Monetary Fund, 1974.

Alexander, Sidney S., 'Effects of a Devaluation on the Trade Balance', *International Monetary Fund Staff Papers*, 2 (April 1952) 263–78.

Aliber, Robert Z., 'Speculation in the Foreign Exchanges: The European Experience, 1919–26', *Yale Economic Essays* (Spring 1962) 197–245.

Aliber, Robert Z., *'Exchange Risk and Corporate International Finance'*, New York, Wiley, 1978.

Argy, Victor, and Kouri, Pentti J. K., 'Sterilization Policies and the Volatility of International Reserves', in Aliber Robert Z. (ed.), *National Monetary Policies and the International Financial System*, Chicago, University of Chicago Press, 1974: 209–30.

Artus, Jacques R., 'Exchange Rate Stability and Managed Floating: The Experience of the Federal Republic of Germany', *International Monetary Fund Staff Papers*, 23 (July 1976) 312–33.

Baffi, Paolo, and Occhiuto, Antonio, 'La Componente Esterna della Liquidita e le Regole della Condotta Monetaria', *Giornale degli Economisti e Annali di Economia*, 19 (Nov.–Dec. 1960) 715–33.

Baffi, Paolo, 'L'evoluzione monetaria in Italia dall'economia di guerra alla convertibilità (1935–58)', in *Studi sulla Moneta*, Milan, Giuffre, 1965.

Baffi, Paolo, 'L'Inflazione in Europa Occidentale e le Monete di Riserva', *Moneta e Credito*, 21 (March 1968) 3–23.

Barone, Enrico, *Principi di Economia Politica*, Rome, Edizioni Atheneum, 1913.

Basevi, Giorgio, and De Grauwe, Paul, 'Vicious and Virtuous Circles: A Theoretical Analysis and a Policy Proposal for Managing Exchange Rates', *European Economic Review*, 10 (Dec. 1977) 277–301.

Bean, Donna, 'International Reserve Flows and Money Market Adjustment: The Japanese Case', in Frenkel, Jacob A., and Johnson,

Harry G. (eds), *The Monetary Approach to the Balance of Payments*, London, Allen & Unwin, 1976: 326–37.

Beccaria, Carlo., *Elementi di Economia Pubblica*, 1754. Reprinted in Collezione Custodi, *Scrittori Classici Italiani di Economia Politica*, 19, Milan, 1804.

Bergstrom, A. R., and Wymer, C. R., 'A Model of Disequilibrium Neoclassical growth and its Application to the United Kingdom' in *Statistical Inference in Continuous Time Economic Models*, Bergstrom, (ed.), A. R., Amsterdam, North Holland Publishing Co., 1976.

Biagioli, Antonello, 'I movimenti di capitali dell'Italia', *Rivista Internazionale di Scienze Sociali*, 83 (May–June 1975) 596–611.

Blejer, Mario, 'Money Prices and the Balance of Payments: The Case of Mexico, 1950–1973', Ph.D. Dissertation, University of Chicago, 1975.

Branson, William H., *Monetary Policy and the New View of International Capital Movements*, Washington, D.C., Brookings Institution, 1970: 235–70.

Bresciani-Turroni, Costantino, *Inflazione Cartacea, Finanza Statale e Corso dei Cambi in Germania*, Trieste, Editore il Circolo di Studi, 1924.

Bresciani-Turroni, Costantino, 'Egypt's Balance of Trade', *Journal of Political Economy*, 42 (June 1934) 371–84.

Bresciani-Turroni, Costantino, *The Economics of Inflation*, London, Allen & Unwin, 1937.

Bresciani-Turroni, Costantino, *Corso di Economia Politica*, Milan, Giuffre, 1954.

Brittain, Bruce, 'Monetary Balance of Payments Theory: Implications and Tests', First National City Bank of New York, 1974.

Brittain, Bruce, and Kumar, Sri, 'Direct Tests of Monetary Balance of Payments Theory', First National City Bank of New York, 1975.

Broggia, Carlo Alberto, *Trattato delle Monete*, Napoli, 1743. Reprinted in Collezione Custodi, *Scrittori Classici Italiani di Economia Politica*, 4 and 5, Milan, 1804.

Cantillon, Richard, *Essai sur la nature du Commerce en général*, London, 1755.

Carli, Gian Rinaldo, 'Dissertazione dell'origine e del Commercio della Moneta, e dei Disordini che Accadono nelle Alterazioni di essa', Venice, 1754. Reprinted in Collezione Custodi, *Scrittori Classici Italiani di Economia Politica*, 20, Milan, 1804.

Carli, Gian Rinaldo, 'Del valore e della Proporzione dei Metalli

Monetati', Lucca, 1760. Reprinted in Collezione Custodi, *Scrittori Classici Italiani di Economia Politica,* 20, Milan, 1804.

Carli, Guido, *Relazione Annuale Banca d'Italia, Considerazioni Finali 1974 and 1973*, Rome, Bank of Italy.

Cassel, Gustav, *Money and Foreign Exchange After 1914*, New York, Macmillan, 1922.

Cattaneo, Carlo, 'Sulle fluttuazioni nella produzione dell'oro' and 'Del credito e della riforma monetaria', Milan, 1839. Reprinted in *Scritti Economici di Carlo Cattaneo*, Bartolino, A., (ed.), Florence, Felice Le Monnier, 1956.

Cesarano, Filippo, 'Monetary Theory in Ferdinando Galani's Della Moneta', *History of Political Economy*, 8 (Fall, 1976) 380–99.

Chiesa, Carlo, 'Una stima dei movimenti di capitali nascosti nel turismo e nelle rimesse degli emigrati', *Contributi alla Ricerca Economica del Servizio Studi della Banca d'Italia*, 4 (June 1975) 7–21.

Chiesa, Gabriella, 'Un modello di disequilibrio dell'economia Italiana', unpublished paper, Confindustria, 1979.

Connolly, Michael, and Taylor, Dean, 'Adjustment to a Devaluation with Money and Nontraded Goods', *Journal of International Economics*, 6 (Aug. 1976) 289–98.

Coghlan, Richard, 'Alternative Portfolio Approaches to Balance of Payments Adjustment', *Scottish Journal of Economics*, 25 (Feb. 1978) 13–28.

Cotula, Franco, 'La Domanda di Moneta, Gruppo per la Politicia Monetaria e Fiscale', unpublished paper, Rome, Bank of Italy, 1970.

Cotula, Franco, and De Stefani, Pietro, '*La politica monetaria in Italia: Istituti e Strumenti*', Bologna, Il Mulino, 1979.

Cristini, Giovanni, 'La Componente estera della Base Monetaria e le 'Regole del Gioco' nei Paesi CEE e negli U.S.A', *Contributi Alla Ricerca Economica*, Rome, Bank of Italy, 1973: 181–209.

Courchene, J. Thomas, and Singh, Karnail, 'The Monetary Approach to the Balance of Payments: An Empirical Analysis for 14 Industrialised Countries', in Parkin, M., and Zis, G. (eds), *Inflation and the World Economy*, Manchester, Manchester University Press, 1976: 189–214.

Dewald, William G., and Johnson, Harry G., 'An Objective Analysis of the Objectives of American Monetary Policy, 1952–1961', in *Banking and Monetary Studies*, Canson, Deane, (ed.), Homewood, Illinois, Irwin, 1963: 171–89.

Di Panfilo, Romeo, and Savona, Paolo, 'Anilisi delle Determinanti della Domanda di Interventi', unpublished paper, Rome, Bank of Italy, 1973.

Dornbusch, Rudiger, 'Devaluation, Relative Prices and the Real Value of Money', Report 7130, Centre for Mathematical Studies in Business and Economics, University of Chicago, 1971. (a)

Dornbusch, Rudiger, 'Notes on Growth and the Balance of Payments', *Canadian Journal of Economics*, 37 (Aug. 1971) 389–95. (b)

Dornbusch, Rudiger, 'Currency Depreciation, Hoarding, and Relative Prices', *Journal of Political Economy*, 81 (Sept. 1973) 893–915. (a)

Dornbusch, Rudiger, 'Devaluation, Money and Non-traded Goods', *American Economic Review*, 68 (Dec. 1973) 871–80. (b)

Dornbusch, Rudiger, 'Real and Monetary Aspects of the Effects of Exchange Rate Changes', in Aliber Robert Z. (ed.), *National Monetary Policies and the International Financial System*, Chicago, University of Chicago Press, 1974: 64–81.

Dornbusch, Rudiger, and Mussa, Michael, 'Consumption, Real Balances and the Hoarding Function', *International Economic Review*, 16 (June 1975) 415–21.

Dornbusch, Rudiger, 'Exchange Rates and Fiscal Policy in a popular Modeal of International Trade', Report 7503, Centre for Mathematical Studies in Business and Economics, University of Chicago, 1975. (a)

Dornbusch, Rudiger, 'A Portfolio Balance Model of the Open Economy', *Journal of Monetary Economics, 1 (Jan. 1975) 3–20.* (b)

Dornbusch, Rudiger, 'Capital Mobility and Portfolio Balance', unpublished paper, University of Chicago, 1975. (c)

Dornbusch, R, 'The theory of Flexible Exchange Rate Regimes and Macro-economic Policy', *Scandinavian Journal of Economics*, 78, 2 (1976) 255–75.

Einaudi, Luigi, 'Rompere il Torchio dei Biglietti', *Corriere della Sera*, November 23, Reprinted in *Il Buongoverno, Saggi di Economia Politica*, Bari, Laterza, 1954: 162–7.

Einaudi, Luigi, *Problemi Economici della Federazione Europea*, Lugano, Nuove Edizioni di Capolago, 1944.

Einaudi, Luigi, *Relazione Annuale Banca d'Italia 1946, Considerazioni Finali.* Rome, Bank of Italy 1946.

Ford, A. G., 'Flexible Exchange rates in Argentina, 1885–1900', *Oxford Economic Papers*, 10 (Oct. 1958) 316–38.

Fratianni, Michele, *Inflazione, Produzione e Politica Economica in Italia*, Milan, Franco Angeli, 1975.

Frankel, Jacob A., 'Adjustment Mechanisms and the Monetary Approach to the Balance of Payments: A Doctrinal Perspective', in *Recent Issues in International Monetary Economics*, Claassen E., and

Salin, P. (eds), Vol. 2 of *Studies in Monetary Economics*. Amsterdam. North Holland Publishing Co., 1976: 29–48. (a)

Frenkel, Jacob A., 'A Dynamic Analysis of the Balance of Payments in a Model of Accumulation', in Frenkel, J. A., and Johnson, Harry G. (eds), *The Monetary Approach to the Balance of Payments*, London, Allen & Unwin, 1976: 109–46. (b)

Frenkel, J. A., 'A Monetary Approach to the Exchange Rate: Doctrinal Aspects and Empirical Evidence', *Scandinavian Journal of Economics*, 78, 2 (1976) 200–24 (c).

Frenkel, J. A., and Johnson, H. G., *'The Monetary Approach to the balance of payments'*, London, Allen & Unwin, 1976.

Frenkel, Jacob A., and Johnson, Harry G., 'The Monetary Approach to the balance of payments: Essential Concepts and Historical Origins', in Frenkel, J. A., and Johnson, H. G. (eds), *The Monetary Approach to the Balance of Payments*, London, Allen & Unwin, 1976.

Frenkel, Jacob A., and Rodriguez, Carlos A., 'Portfolio Equilibrium and the Balance of Payments: A Monetary Approach', *American Economic Review*, 70 (Sept. 1975) 674–88.

Friedlaender, Ann F., 'Macro Policy Goals in the Postwar Period: A Study in Revealed Preference', *Quarterly Journal of Economics*, 87 (Feb. 1973) 25–43.

Froyen, Richard T., 'A Test of the Endogeneity of Monetary Policy', *Journal of Econometrics*, 2 (May 1974) 175–88.

Galiani, Ferdinando, *Della Moneta*, Naples, 1750. Reprinted in Collezioni Custodi, *Scrittori Classici Italiani di Economia Politica*, 10 and 11, Milan 1804.

Gandolfo, G., *Mathematical Methods and Models of Economic Dynamics*, Amsterdam, North Holland Publishing Co., 1971: 240.

Gandolfi, Arthur E., and Lothian, James R., 'A Comparison of Price Movements Among Countries and States', First National City Bank of New York, 1975.

Genberg, Hans, 'Aspects of the Monetary Approach to the Balance of Payments Theory: An Empirical Study of Sweden', Ph.D. dissertation, University of Chicago, 1974. Also in Frenkel, J. A., and Johnson, Harry G. (eds), *The Monetary Approach to the Balance of Payments*, London, Allen & Unwin, 1976: 298–325.

Genberg, H., 'World inflation and the Small Open Economy', *Swedish Industrial Publications*, Stockholm, 1975.

Genberg, Hans, and Swoboda, K. Alexander, 'Worldwide Inflation Under the Dollar Standard', unpublished paper, Geneva, Graduate Institute of International Studies, January 1977.

Genovesi, Antonio, *Lezioni di Economia Civile*, Parte Seconda 1765. Reprinted in Collezioni Custodi, *Scrittori Classici Italiani di Economia Politica*, 16, Milan, 1804.

Genovesi, Antonio, 'Opuscoli di Economia Politica', 1765. Reprinted in Collezioni Custodi, *Scrittori Classici Italiani di Economia Politica*, 16, Milan, 1804.

Girton, Lance, and Roper, Don, 'A Monetary Model of Exchange Market Pressure Applied to the Postwar Canadian Experience', *American Economic Review*, 67 (Sept. 1977) 537–48.

Godley, W., and Cripps, F., 'Demand Inflation and Economic Policy', *London and Cambridge Economic Bulletin*, 84, reprinted in *The Times*, January 22 and 23, 1974.

Godley, W., and Cripps, F., 'A Formal Analysis of the Cambridge Economic Policy Group Model', *Economica*, 43 (Nov. 1976) 335–48.

Guitian, Manuel, 'The Balance of Payments as a Monetary Phenomenon: Empirical Evidence, Spain, 1955–1971', in Frenkel, J. A., and Johnson, Harry G. (eds) *The Monetary Approach to the Balance of Payments*, London, Allen & Unwin, 1976: 338–56.

Haberler, Gottfried, 'The Markets for Foreign Exchanges and the Stability of the Balance of Payments: A Theoretical Analysis', *Kyklos*, 3 (1949) 193–218.

Harberger, Arnold C., 'Currency Depreciation, Income and the Balance of Trade', *Journal of Political Economy*, 58 (Feb. 1950) 47–60.

Heller, Robert H., *International Trade Theory and Empirical Evidence*, Englewood Cliffs, N.J., Prentice Hall, 1968: 60–87.

Heller, Robert H., 'International Reserves and Worldwide Inflation', *International Monetary Fund Staff Papers*, 23 (March 1976) 61–87.

Hodgson, J. S., 'Analysis of Floating Exchange Rates: The Dollar-Sterling Rate 1919–25', *Southern Economic Journal*, 39 (Oct. 1972) 249–57.

Hume, David, *On The Balance of Trade*. Reprinted in *International Finance*, Cooper, R. N. (ed.), Harmondsworth Publishing Co., 1969: 25–37.

International Monetary Fund, *International Financial Statistics*, 1971 and 1973 Supplements, and various succeeding issues.

International Monetary Fund, *The Monetary Approach to the Balance of Payments*, Washington, D.C., 1977.

ISCO, Istituto Nazionale per lo Studio della Congiuntura, *Conti Economici Trimestrali*, Rome, 1977.

Johnson, Harry G., 'Towards a General Theory of the Balance of Payments', in Johnson, Harry G. (ed.), *International Trade and Economic Growth*, London, Allen & Unwin, 1958: 153–68.

Johnson, Harry G., 'The Monetary Approach to the Balance of Payments Theory', in Connolly, Michael B., and Swoboda, Alexander K. (eds), *International Trade and Money*, London, Allen & Unwin, 1973: 206–24.

Johnson, Harry G., 'Major Issues in Monetary Economics', *Oxford Economic Papers* 26 (July 1974) 212–25.

Johnson, Harry G., *Inflation and the Monetarist Controversy*, Amsterdam, North Holland Publishing Co., 1972.

Johnson, Harry G.,'Elasticity, Absorption, Keynesian Multiplier, Keynesian Policy and Monetary Approaches to Devaluation Theory: A Simple Geometric Exposition', *American Economic Review*, 66 (June 1976).

Johnson, Peter D., 'Money and Economic Activity in the Open Economy: The United Kingdom, 1880–1970', *Journal of Political Economy*, 84 (Dec. 1976) 979–1012.

Johnson, Peter D., and Kierzkowski, I., 'The Balance of Payments: An Analytic Exercise', *Manchester School of Economic and Social Studies*, 2 (June 1975) 105–33.

Keran, Michael, 'Monetary Policy and Business Cycles in Postwar Japan', in *Varieties of Monetary Experience*, Maiselman, David (ed.), Chicago, University of Chicago Press, 1970: 163–248.

Knight, Malcolm D., and Wymer, Clifford R., 'A Macroeconomic Model of the United Kingdom', *International Monetary Fund Staff Papers*, 25 (Dec. 1978) 742–78.

Kouri, Pentti J. K., and Porter, Michael G., 'International Capital Flows and Portfolio Equilibrium', *Journal of Political Economy*, 82 (June 1974) 443–67.

Laffer, Arthur, 'Monetary Policy and the Balance of Payments', *Journal of Money, Credit and Banking*, 4 (Feb. 1972) 13–22.

Machlup, Fritz, *International Trade and the National Income Multiplier*, Philadelphia, Blakiston, 1943.

Masera, R. S., 'The Budget Deficit, and the Interaction between Money, the Exchange Rate and Prices: The Italian Experience in the 1970s', paper presented at the seminar on 'Recent Developments in Western Economics', Brasenose College, Oxford, July 4–7, 1976.

Metzler, Lloyd A., 'Wealth, Saving and the Rate of Interest', *Journal of Political Economy*, 59 (Apr. 1951) 93–116.

Montanari, Geminiano, 'Della Moneta, Trattato Mercantile', 1680.

Reprinted in Collezione Custodi, *Scrittori Classici Italiani di Economia Politica*, 3, Milan, 1804.

Montanari, Geminiano, 'Breve Trattato del Valore delle Monete in Tutti gli Stati', 1680. Reprinted in Collezione Custodi, *Scrittori Classici Italiani di Economia Politica*, 3., Milan, 1804.

Mundell, Robert A., *International Economics*, New York, Macmillan, 1968.

Mundell, Robert A., *Monetary Theory: Inflation, Interest and Growth in the World Economy*, Pacific Palisades, Goodyear, 1971.

Mussa, Michael, 'A Monetary Approach to the Balance of Payments Analysis', *Journal of Money, Credit and Banking* (Aug. 1974) 333–51.

Myhrman, Johan, 'Balance of Payments Adjustment and Portfolio Theory: A Survey', paper presented at the Third Paris-Dauphine Conference on Money and Monetary Problems, March 28–30, 1974.

Nield, R., 'The Case for a Change in Fiscal Policy: Mid-1973', *London and Cambridge Economic Bulletin* 83, reprinted in *The Times*, July 19 and 20, 1973.

Pantaleoni, Maffeo. *Principi di Economia Pura*, Florence, Barbera, 1894.

Pareto, Vilfredo, *Cours d'Economie Politique*, Lausanne, F. Rouge, 1896.

Parkin, Michael, 'Inflation, the Balance of Payments, Domestic Credit Expansion, and Exchange Rate Adjustment', in Aliber, Robert Z. (ed.), *National Monetary Policies and the International Financial System*, Chicago, University of Chicago Press, 1974: 49–63.

Prais, S. J., 'Mathematical Notes on the Quantity Theory of Money in an Open Economy', *International Monetary Fund Staff Papers*, 8 (Jan. 1961) 1–28.

Ranuzzi de Bianchi, Paolo, 'La Funzione di Preferenza della Autorita Monetaria in Italia dal 1958 al 1969', *Moneta e Credito*, 24 (June 1971) 157–70.

Robinson, Joan, 'The Foreign Exchanges', in Ellis, H. S., and Metzler, L. A. (eds), *Readings in the Theory of International Trade*, Philadelphia, Blakiston, 1949: 83–103.

Rodriguez, Carlos, A., 'Money and Wealth in an Open Economy Income Expenditure Model', in Frenkel, J. A., and Johnson, Harry G. (eds), *The Monetary Approach to the Balance of Payments*, London, Allen & Unwin, 1976: 222–36.

Rueber, G. L., 'The Objectives of Canadian Monetary Policy, 1949–1961: Empirical Trade Offs and the Reaction Function of the

Monetary Authorities', *Journal of Political Economy*, 72 (Apr. 1964) 109–32.

Salvemini, Maria Teresa, 'La moneta nella politica di finanziamento del disavanzo', 'Saggi brevi di economia a cura della Banca Commerciale Italiana', Milan, Giuffre, 1974.

Sanssapour, Cyrus, and Sheen, Jeffery, R., 'A Comparison of Money and Economic Activity in France and West Germany: 1959–73', paper prepared for the SSRC Ford Foundation Conference on 'Macroeconomic Policy and Adjustment in Open Economics', Fenhams Hall, Ware, England, 28 April–1 May, 1976.

Sartorelli, Carlo, 'Gli Acquisti a Sostegno delle Quotazioni dei Titoli a Reddito Fisso', unpublished paper, Rome, Bank of Italy, 1973.

Savona, Paolo, 'Inflazione Moneta e Bilancia dei Pagamenti', *Rivista di Politica Economica*, 65 (May 1975) 613–36. (a)

Savona, Paolo, *La Sovranita Monetaria*, Rome, Buffetti, 1975. (b)

Schumpeter, J. A., *History of Economic Analysis*, London, Oxford University Press, 1954.

Serra, Antonio, 'Breve Trattato delle Cause che Possono far Abbandonare li Regni di oro e D'argento dove non Sono Miniere', 1613. Reprinted in Collezione Custodi, *Scrittori Classici Italiani di Economia Politica*, Milan, 1803.

Staley, Charles, E., 'Hume and Viner on the International Adjustment Mechanism', *History of Political Economy*, 8 (Summer 1976) 252–65.

Sylos, Labini Paolo, 'Competition: The Product Markets in the market and the State', in *Essays in honour of Adam Smith*, Wilson, Thomas, and Skinner, Andrew (eds) Oxford, Clarendon Press, 1976: 200–32.

Swoboda, Alexander K., 'The Eurodollar Market: An Interpretation', *Essays in International Finance*, 64 (Feb. 1968).

Swoboda, Alexander K., 'Reserve Policies, Currency Preferences, and International Adjustment', *Yale Economic Essays* 10 (Spring 1970) 83–121.

Swoboda, Alexander K., 'Monetary Policy under Fixed Exchange Rates: Effectiveness, the Speed of Adjustment and Proper Use', *Economica*, 40 (May 1973) 136–54.

Swoboda, Alexander K., 'Monetary Approaches to the Transmission and Generation of World Wide Inflation', Unpublished manuscript, Graduate Institute of International Studies, 1975.

Tullio, Giuseppe, 'I movimenti di capitali dell'Italia in regime di cambi fissi: una ristima del modello di Kouri e Porter', *Contributi alla Ricerca Economica del Servizio Studi della Banca d'Italia*, 7 (Dec. 1977) 165–81.

Tullio, Giuseppe, 'The Fluctuations of the Price of Italian Banknotes in Zurich: an Econometric Analysis (Feb. 1973–Dec. 1975)', *Kyklos* 31 (Sept. 1978) 462–74.

Tullio, Giuseppe, 'Monetary Equilibrium and Balance of Payments Adjustment: An Empirical Test of the U.S. Balance of Payments (1951–73)', *Journal of Money, Credit and Banking*, 11 (Feb. 1979) 68–79. (a)

Tullio, Giuseppe, 'An Empirical Note on Relative Monetary Expansion and Depreciation: The case of the Lira-Swiss France Exchange Rate, (Feb. 1973–Dec. 1976)', *European Economic Review* (Feb. 1979) 91–100. (b)

Tullio, Giuseppe, '*Moneta, Cambio e bilancia dei pagamenti: una teoria dell' aggustamento internazionale. Origini storiche e verifiche empiriche per l'Italia e gli Stati Uniti*', *Saggi Brevi di Economia*, a cura della Banca Commerciale Italiana, Comunità, Milan, 1979. (c)

Tullio Giuseppe, 'Demand Management and Exchange Rate Policy in a Vicious Circle Country: Lessons from the Italian experience' Document of the International Monetary Fund, DM/80/59, Washington D.C, September 1980.

Ujiie, J., 'Dynamic Aspects of Monetary Policy and the Balance of Payments', Ph.D. dissertation, University of Chicago, 1975.

Verri, Pietro, 'Meditazioni sull' Economia Politica', 1772. Reprinted in Collezioni Custodi, *Scrittori Classici Italiani di Economia Politica*, 22, Milan, 1804.

Vicarelli, F., 'L'esportazione di banconote nell'esperienza Italiana dell'ultimo decennio: un'analisi quantitativa', *Studi Economici*, 25 (May-Aug. 1970) 322–47.

Williamson, Jeffrey, *American Growth and the Balance of Payments: 1820-1913*, Chapel Hill, N.C., University of North Carolina Press, 1964.

Zecher, J. Richard, 'Monetary Equilibrium and International Reserve Flows in Australia', *Journal of Finance*, 19 (Dec. 1974) 1523–30.

Index

Absorption approach, xiv–xvii
Alexander, Sidney, xvi
Approach
  absorption, xiv–xvii
  elasticity, xiv–xvi
  monetary
    assumptions and implications, 3–22
    to the balance of payments, 31–7
    to the exchange rate, 85–9
Arbitrage, 10–11
  and the law of one price, 10–11
  and the natural distribution of money, 11–12

Baffi, Paolo, xv, 54, 58, 60
Balance of payments
  crises in Italy, 38, 41–4, 61–2
  definition in Italy, 111
  fluctuations in Italy, 31–51
  monetary approach to, 3–22, 31–7
Bank notes, exchange rate for, 87–91
Bank of Italy, xviii, xix, 31–2, 36, 51, 55, 57, 59–60, 62–4, 72–85, 92–3, 98
Barone, Enrico, xvii, 10–12, 14–15, 21
Basevi, Giorgio, 95
Beccaria, Carlo, xvii, 11, 13
Bergstrom, R., 80
Biagioli, Antonello, 113
Blejer, Mario, 56
Bond
  issues in Italy, 65–8
  purchases in Italy, 68
Bresciani-Turroni, Costantino, xi, xv, 1, 4, 10–11, 13, 18–19, 54
Broggia, Carlo Alberto, 10, 16

Cable transfers, exchange rate for, 87–91
Cambridge view, xiv, 98–101
Capital account
  effect of monetary policy on, 101–4
Carli, Gian Rinaldo, 9, 17–18
Cassel, Gustav, xiv
Cattaneo, Carlo, 9, 20
Ceilings on bank loans, 60–2
Cesarano, Filippo, 29
Chiesa, Carlo, 112
Chiesa, Gabriella, xx, 56
Claims of Bank of Italy
  on commercial banks, 76–9
  on government, 75–7
Commercial banks
  ceilings on loans, 60–2
  controls on net foreign asset position, 42, 60–3
  controls on portfolio composition, 59–64
Controls
  on capital flows, 42, 101, 110
  on net foreign asset position of commercial banks, 42, 60–3
  on portfolio composition of commercial banks, 59–64
Cripps, F., 113
Current account
  effect of monetary policy on, 101–9

Debasement of a currency, 6, 15–16, 28
De Cindio, Giovanni, 95
De Grauwe, Paul, 95

Demand for money, 7–9, 18, 21
 in Italy, 32, 45–6, 85–6, 101
Devaluation
 effects of, 5–7, 15–16
 neutrality of, xvii, 7, 15–16
Direct expenditure effect, 2, 6, 19–22, 25–7
Domestic assets of Bank of Italy, 74–5, 77–80
Dornbusch, Rudiger, xvii, 7, 95

Elasticity
 approach, xiv–xvi
 income elasticity of demand for money in Italy, 45
 interest elasticity of demand for money in Italy, 45
Exchange Rate Crisis of 1976, 92–3

Financial markets
 developments in Italy, 65–70
Financing Requirement, *see* Treasury Financing Requirement
Foreign Trade Multiplier Theory, xvi
Franc, exchange rate of lira and Swiss franc, 89–94
Frenkel, Jacob, xx, 6

Galiani, Ferdinando, 8, 12, 15, 19, 28
Gandolfo, Giancarlo, 29
Genberg, Hans 28, 41
Girton, Lance, 95
Godley, W., 113
Gold
 Exchange standard, 23–4
 Standard, 25
Gresham Law, 6, 16–18

Haberler, Gottfried, xv
Harberger, Arnold, xvi
Hoarding, 28
Hume, David, xi, xiv, 2, 6, 26, 28

IFS, *see* International Financial Statistics
Independence of monetary policy and the size of countries, 17, 23–5
 in Italy, 35–7, 72–80
International Financial Statistics, 51–2, 72, 94–5, 112
International Monetary Fund, xv, 51–2, 72, 94–5, 112
International Reserves, effect of monetary policy on, 23–7;
 see also Monetary policy, effects on the balance of payments
Interventions
 in bond market, 55, 57, 81
 in foreign exchange market, 84–5, 88–9, 109
Italian
 Agricultural trade deficit, 5
 Balance of payments
  crises, 38, 41–4, 61–2
  definition, 111
  fluctuations, 31–49
 Capital account, 102–4
 Current account, 98–111
 Economic thought, 3–22
 Financial Market Developments, 65–70
 Monetary Policy, 37–42, 58–64, 70–82
 Money supply process, 57–64

Johnson, Harry, xv, xvi, xx, 4, 8, 14, 16, 30
Jonson, Peter, xx, 80

Keynes, John Maynard, 21
Knight, Malcolm, xx, 56, 80
Kouri, Pentti, 113

Law of one price, 10–11

Machlup, Fritz, xvi
Marshall-Lerner condition, xv
Monetary approach
 assumptions and implications, 3–22
 to balance of payments, 31–7
 to exchange rate, 85–9
Monetary base, domestic component of, 14–15, 23–7
 in Italy, *see* Domestic assets of Bank of Italy

Monetary policy
  effects of,
    on the balance of payments, xix, 3, 6, 16–19, 36–42, 47–9
    on the capital account, 101–4
    on the current account, 104–9
    on the exchange rate, xix, 15, 18–19, 89–93
    on the level of foreign exchange reserves, 23–5
  objectives of, in Italy, 70–81
Money
  demand for, 7–9, 18, 21
  in Italy, 32, 45–6, 85–6, 101
  market and the balance of payments, 4–6
  supply process in Italy, 57–64
Montanari, Geminiano, 10, 12, 16
Multiplier of foreign trade, *see* Foreign trade multiplier
Mundell, Robert, xv, xvii, 3–4, 7, 16, 18, 30
Muss, Michael, xvii, 4

Natural distribution of money, 3, 11, 12
Neutrality of devaluation, xvii, 7, 15, 16
Neutralization of international reserve flows, 31, 36–7, 58, 60, 71, 73, 75, 81, 83
Nield, R. 113
Non-traded goods, 19–22, 25–7

Objectives of monetary policy, *see* Monetary policy
Ohlin, Bertil, 21
Oil crisis
  effect on balance of payments, 51, 55–6
  effect on exchange rate, 88–9, 95

Pantaleoni, Maffeo, 11, 17–18
Pareto, Vilfredo, 3, 9, 11–12, 18, 20–1
Porter, Michael, 113
Prais, S. J., xvii, 3, 13
Price specie flow, xiv, 2, 6, 19–22, 25–7
Purchasing power parity, xiv, 86

Reaction function, 37–42, 70–80
Real balance effect, xvi
Reparations (German), 21
Reverse causation, 37, 72, 85, 97
Rodriguez, Carlos, 95
Roper, Don, 95

Sartorelli, Carlo, 57
Saussapour, Cyrus, 80
Savona, Paolo, 57
Schumpter, Joseph, 13
Self-adjusting nature of balance of payments disequilibria, 3–4, 13–14;
  see also Stability of equilibrium
Serra, Antonio, xi, xvii, 1, 7–8, 13, 15, 21
Sheen, Jeffry, 80
Silver, gold, price of, 20
Small country assumption, 11, 17, 19, 32–3
Speed of adjustment to money market disturbances
  of prices, 15
  of Italian balance of payments, 36–42, 47–9
  of Italian capital account, 103–4
  of Italian current account, 104–9
  of Italian exchange rate, 89–93
Spread between the lira and Swiss franc exchange rates, 87–91
Stability of equilibrium, 12–14
Staley, Charles, 28
Sterilization of international reserve flows, *see* Neutralization
Stocks *vs* flows, xvi, 9, 13, 46–7
Swiss franc, exchange rate, 89–94
Swoboda, Alexander, 3, 102, 111

Trade balance, effect on exchange rate, 88–90
Traded goods, 19–22
Transmission of world inflation, 41
Transport costs and the law of one price, 10
Treasury
  Financing Requirement

and the balance of payments, 36–41
and the capital account, 101–4
and the current account, 101–9
and the lira exchange rate crisis of 1976, 92–3
and the money supply process, 71–80
Bills, 64, 70
Two-stage least-square estimates
of Italian balance of payments, 35–42
of reaction function, 35–42

Ujiie, J., 71
University of Chicago, xi, xiii, xv

Verri, Pietro, xvii, 13–14, 22

Walras' law, 4, 28, 32, 86
Wedge between income and expenditure, xvi, xvii, 5–6, 13, 22, 28
Wymer, Clifford, xx, 56, 80